T0350528

Additional praise for *Start-Up Secure*

"It's rare to see a cybersecurity guide of any kind that is relevant, current, and, most importantly, cogent and accessible. Chris Castaldo has not only produced such a guide but has tailored it for an audience who has never before received such wisdom in a digestible manner – the startup community. Startups are notoriously fast-moving, and Castaldo's book keeps up with them, showing them the types of practical security controls they need throughout their rapid journey to whatever exit strategy they envision."

– Allan Alford, CISO/CTO, TrustMAPP and Host of the
The Cyber Ranch Podcast

"*Start-Up Secure* offers important insights and advice in an area that is often overlooked by entrepreneurs. Cybersecurity has emerged as a critical competency for businesses, and this trend will likely continue or accelerate. The guidance provided in these pages will save founders from making preventable mistakes in multiple dimensions, from technical security decisions to avoiding unreasonable contract language. The wisdom shared by Chris is hard-learned, and a valuable addition to any entrepreneur's thought process."

– Paul Ihme, co-founder, Soteria

"Cybersecurity is often thought of as too intimidating or complex for the layperson to comprehend. Chris Castaldo's book, *Start-Up Secure*, seeks to take the mystery out of succeeding at cybersecurity. His straightforward and direct approach serves as an essential guide to starting out on the right foot with your security program. It is accessible and actionable and I would recommend it to anyone seeking to tackle cybersecurity, the most important business challenge of our time."

– Brian Markham, CISO, EAB Global Inc.

Start-Up Secure

Start-Up Secure

Baking Cybersecurity into Your
Company from Founding to Exit

CHRIS CASTALDO

WILEY

Library of Congress Cataloging-in-Publication Data is Available:

ISBN 978-1-119-70073-9 (Hardback)
ISBN 978-1-119-70074-6 (ePDF)
ISBN 978-1-119-70075-3 (ePub)

Cover Design: Wiley
Cover Image: © deepadesigns/Shutterstock

SKY10026092_040121

To my wife, daughter, and son, you have made reality better than the dream.

Contents

Foreword

"Connect"

I connected with Chris years ago. In classic Chris fashion: he shared a thoughtful cybersecurity insight on LinkedIn and our mutual friend connected the dots between us. While meeting him was great, little did I realize that simple connection was going to lead to years of friendship and learning.

Cybersecurity has been in such a constant state of flux that many companies still don't know how to write a chief information security officer (CISO) job description; they don't know what a CISO does in their day-to-day job. You will find CISOs as heads of IT, internal pentesters, security engineers, writing compliance reports, negotiating legal terms, reporting to any C-suite role, and some taking primarily customer-facing responsibilities.

There is little question that the security role is still in an early stage in its evolution. With all of that confusion, it is no wonder that resource-constrained start-ups and founders have no idea how to proactively build a security program. And with a start-up's demands to prioritize time, opportunity, and resources, it's no surprise to find start-ups with no security programs at all.

The reality is that as the world evolves and more business becomes increasingly digital, the security bar is rising for all vendors. Every customer that trusts a vendor with its resources (i.e., financials, customer data) wants to know that their sensitive information is being handled safely; something they know the bigger vendors are likely working on.

Luckily, start-ups are smaller targets for attackers and typically have much less legacy risk to accept. This results in high ROI, low-hanging fruit opportunities for start-ups, and large deltas in security preparedness between early stage start-ups. Coupled with the fast-paced, leading-edge value that a start-up can provide a customer, building security from the beginning is an exciting possibility.

Chris's dedication to learning and to helping the security ecosystem has been incredible to see over the years. This book is yet another example of his efforts to take his lessons learned as a CISO for different-sized companies and to help others. With this book, founders will begin to understand the necessary fundamentals of securing a start-up.

Meeting Chris years ago kicked off an awesome learning opportunity on the day-to-day dynamics of taking on a security leadership role at a fast-growing company. I'm likewise excited for readers to discover this book and to journey deeper into the world of security for start-ups.

Cheers,
Will Lin
Co-Founder & Partner
ForgePoint Capital
Cybersecurity VC

Preface

M OST BOOKS END WITH A QUOTE from a famous source; I am starting with one. In his book *The 7 Habits of Highly Effective People*, Stephen Covey states "The main thing is to keep the main thing the main thing." This should apply to your start-up and how you should view every suggestion in this book. Every cybersecurity choice you make should, at the end of the day, be to enhance whatever it is you are building. From getting a better product out the door to high customer satisfaction from the services you provide. Don't lose sight.

There are a lot of topics covered in this book and cybersecurity taken as a whole can be overwhelming. That's why there is an entire industry built around it. As you read through this book, always keep in mind what is right for your start-up and your customers. You don't need to implement all the things we discuss in this book from day one or even by day one thousand. But you should understand the important trade-offs by the end of this book.

Just knowing those trade-offs then allows you to prioritize what is right for your start-up and allows you to keep the main thing the main thing. A great example is a security incident and event management (SIEM)[1] solution, which is something you most likely won't need until after the validation phase, maybe even beyond the growth phase. I hope to provide you with the right know-how and understanding to intelligently make those decisions.

Of course, you are not in this alone. Your fellow founders, board members, venture capital (VC) advisory board, customers, peers, and vendors are all sources to validate your overall cybersecurity plan. Utilize the free resources that want to help and see your start-up succeed.

▓ WHY WRITE THIS BOOK?

Cybersecurity is now a requirement for every company in the world, regardless of size or industry. Regulations and laws at the state, national, and international levels are being created at a faster rate. Constituents expect their elected officials to not only investigate the massive data breaches we've seen over the years, but also that those politicians do something about it. It is especially important for start-ups.

This book was written to be the go-to source for start-up founders, entrepreneurs, leaders, and individual contributors. There is no expectation for companies because of a lack of technical prowess or even experience as a cybersecurity professional. Accounting is an obvious part of all business, as is cybersecurity, and not everyone can be expected to be a certified public accountant (CPA) or an offensive security certified professional (OSCP).[2]

I will walk you through the sometimes chaotic and confusing world of working with cybersecurity professionals (and trying to be one yourself!), dealing with industry-specific regulations and the almost infinite supply of cybersecurity vendors.

I wrote this book because there are hundreds of books, studies, and white papers on cybersecurity and best practices but nothing speaking directly to founders and start-ups. There are even more books about start-ups and for entrepreneurs, yet not a single one mentions building your company in a secure way. The Kauffman Foundation estimated 530,000 new businesses were created every month in the United States during 2015,[3] which translates to 530,000 new possible targets every month with no ability for them all to hire the experienced cybersecurity professional required to securely run a business today.

Many hiring reports indicate we are currently in a cybersecurity hiring crisis.[4] However, that fact should not prevent any organization from developing and implementing a risk-based and right-sized cybersecurity strategy regardless of the industry they operate in.

This book won't create a new framework or standard, but will translate those that exist into a commonsense selection for entrepreneurs, business leaders, and individual contributors. There is no wrong framework or standard that you could select, but not adopting one will certainly spell disaster for any organization, start-up, or 100-year-old organization. A phrase I vividly remember from my time in the Army deployed to Iraq that sums this up is "get off the X"; regardless of the decision, not making one is typically always wrong.

This book is the culmination of my experience of over 20 years in cybersecurity at start-ups, global tech companies, the National Security Agency, and US military. Since I started this preface with a favorite quote I'd like to close with one that I feel sums up how this book came about. In Nassim Nicholas Taleb's book *Antifragile* he writes, "I write with my scars." I cannot agree more. Without spending many years doing this work and without the support of many professionals that have helped me along the way this book would not be possible. I hope that my experience helps you start-up secure.

NOTES

1. A security incident and event management tool is a system that ingests, processes, correlates, stores, and sometimes takes action on security log events from your systems. These systems can be your laptop, servers running in your cloud infrastructure, or even other security tools.
2. The "offensive security certified professional" is an intense certification that requires hands-on testing of an individual's skills of advanced penetration testing techniques. It is one of the more difficult certifications to achieve.
3. http://www.kauffman.org/~/media/kauffman_org/research %20reports%20and%20covers/2015/05/kauffman_index_start-up_ activity_national_trends_2015.pdf
4. http://www.csoonline.com/article/3075293/leadership-management/cybersecurity-recruitment-in-crisis.html

Acknowledgments

THANK YOU TO EVERYONE who has helped shape who I am over my career. This book absolutely would not have happened without your impact on my life.

Will Lin: I felt I would need an entire chapter to give you proper credit – you have shaped and changed my career and life in ways I may not even know yet.

Richard Seiersen: Thank you for writing one of my favorite books – if not for you, this book most likely would not have happened. I am in debt to your generosity.

Anne Marie Zettlemoyer: Your counsel has been priceless and I feel so very fortunate to call you a friend. Thank you for making me feel included.

Chris Cottrell: I am so thankful for and miss our long walks around the building and for you being a sounding board for my crazy career aspirations I was probably in over my head on. And most of all I value your trust in me. I hope we get to work together again. I am also thankful for [redacted].

Bridgett Nuxoll: You taught me more about cybersecurity than almost anyone. I thought I was the mentor but I was definitely the mentee. And I will always buy Crane & Co.

Jeff Dewberry: I sleep soundly every night knowing you are providing the blanket of freedom our country enjoys.

Yael Nagler: I can't find the words to express how appreciative I am to know you and benefit from your friendship and always accurate advice.

Koos Lodewijkx: Your mentorship has been a huge influence on this book, and while I might never be able to repay that debt, I hope I can at least pay it forward.

Ryan Naraine: Thank you for giving me my first break on a podcast and always being the voice of reason.

Kevin O'Brien: Your feedback has helped make this book even more valuable for the founders that will read it.

Paul Ihme: I appreciate your honesty, feedback, and friendship all these years. I feel lucky to have "come up" together from our days in the government.

Brian Markham: Thank you for making time for me and giving me your valuable experience to make this book a resource for founders. Who knew I'd gain a great friend from one interview?

Gary Hayslip: Thank you for your advice and support. You are always setting the example for cybersecurity leaders and I'm fortunate to continue learning from you.

Allan Alford: Your willingness to always help others is an inspiration to me. Thank you for the honest feedback.

Harold Moss: Thank you for your sound judgment and for leading by example.

Ganesh Pai: Your advice as a founder has been instrumental in helping my audience and giving other founders the critical information they need.

Masha Sedova: Thank you so much for your time and always putting users first. You are truly changing cybersecurity for the better.

Michael Piacente: Your kindness and thoughtfulness when giving your time is a gift. I still remember our first phone call that felt like I was talking to a longtime friend.

Sinan Eren: Thank you for your perspective as a serial founder and all that you have done and do for the cybersecurity community.

Chris Berry: Thank you for being the type of leader someone can aspire to be and teaching me to "ask for forgiveness, not permission." It has served me well over my entire career.

John Scilieri: Your friendship and mentorship over the years helped me make all the right decisions. Thank you for the copy of *The Obstacle Is the Way*, which motivated me to take a risk that paid off and opened my eyes to Stoicism.

Eric Kough: You gave my resume on Monster.com a chance and opened countless doors for me. I'm forever in debt.

Joe Karolchik: It was a privilege to have you as a leader and mentor to learn from.

Victor Goltsman: I'm so grateful for the opportunity I had to work with you, and I try to apply every day what I learned from you.

Security Tinkerers: Thank you to each and every one of you. I am extremely fortunate to be in your company.

About the Author

Chris Castaldo is an industry-recognized chief information security officer (CISO) and expert in building cybersecurity programs for start-ups. Chris's cybersecurity experience stretches over 20 years in start-ups, Fortune 1000s, and the US Government. He has scaled cybersecurity programs and teams from the ground up, and he also advises start-ups. Chris is a US Army veteran and a Visiting Fellow at the National Security Institute at George Mason University's Antonin Scalia Law School.

Introduction

ABOUT THIS BOOK

Chapter 1 will discuss and get you comfortable with building a minimally viable cybersecurity program for a minimally viable product. You don't need to start with National Security Agency (NSA) level security on day one, and most founders reading this book won't even need it the day they ring the opening bell.

Chapter 2 will help you think through and build your cybersecurity roadmap regardless of where you are starting in the start-up life cycle. While it may seem out of order – why wouldn't you plan your roadmap first? – not everyone starts at the point of needing a roadmap, with a defined and documented strategy. If you are a month into building your minimally viable product (MVP) and just received your legal documents officially forming your company, a three-year cybersecurity roadmap is going to take up time and then sit on the shelf.

Chapter 3 is, in my opinion, the most important chapter in this book. If you read one chapter only, make it this one. Your credentials, which make up a username and password, are your keys to your digital self. These are most critical to protect as they underpin nearly all other systems in a cybersecurity program.

Chapter 4 will explore the ever-changing world of antivirus that began nearly 40 years ago and is now called endpoint detection and response (EDR) or endpoint protection platform (EPP). EDR and EPP is an important layer to your cybersecurity program, one that might be difficult to delay beyond the formation phase of your start-up.

Chapter 5 tackles the necessary evil that is our office network, how we connect to the Internet. It makes all of this possible and is also first to be blamed when we can't load our favorite cat video on our office Wi-Fi network.

Chapter 6 we soar into the sky and take a look at the clouds. It is nearly impossible to not use a cloud-based product today and as a founder there is a very good chance you are building a cloud-based product or will use them to scale your start-up.

Chapter 7 covers the actual basics and predecessor to all of this, information technology (IT).

Chapter 8 covers an equally critical topic to Chapter 3: hiring. Making your first cybersecurity hire is a high-impact decision for your start-up. The wrong hire can have disastrous consequences. And making sure you know what you are actually looking for, being honest with yourself and founders, will pay back dividends. Cybersecurity is one of the most competitive fields for jobs and has been for nearly a decade now.

Chapter 9 is a personal favorite of mine. Not everyone enjoys the negotiating challenges of working with a customer's general counsel on terms and conditions, or arguing the auditor's definitions of "was." Being compliant can sometimes mean you can or cannot do business in an industry, country, or with a specific business. This is a chapter you shouldn't skip.

Chapter 10 continues and builds on Chapter 9 and dives specifically into government law and industry regulations. These, much like being compliant with a legal agreement, can stop a start-up in its tracks or open the doors to prospective partner, acquirers and customers.

Chapter 11 will prepare you for the day when people ask you if your product is secure and how you protect their data. It's a good idea to start thinking about these answers now and then look at your answers and verify that you are actually doing that. Someone will eventually want to audit you. Being ready to comfortably and confidently talk about your cybersecurity program will build a lot of trust with investors, customers, and partners.

Chapter 12 will discuss the inevitable data breaches. They are a part of doing business today and we build our cybersecurity programs to the antifragile so we improve when they happen.

Chapter 13 dives further into the technical needs for start-ups that are developing a technical solution, and covers baking cybersecurity into the product you are building, not just your start-up.

Chapter 14 looks at outside risks of doing business today. Third-party vendors, really any vendor, you use will bring some risk to your business. The reward must simply outweigh that risk. This chapter will help you understand how to quickly evaluate that risk.

Chapter 15 will bring us back to where we started and set you and your co-founders on the way to building a secure start-up.

HOW TO USE THIS BOOK

This book is written specifically for founders to take immediate and continuous actions in their start-up to bake in cybersecurity. After each chapter, I will summarize the contents and highlights of the most critical takeaways. Additionally, there will be action plans that you can take immediately and as your start-up scales to implement those suggestions.

These plans will be broken out into generalized phases in your start-up journey from founding to exit. Obviously, not every company takes the same path, so specific catalysts will be mentioned and grouped in a way that may seem contradictory.

1. Formation
   a. One to three founders
   b. No additional full-time staff
   c. Angel or friends and family or bootstrap funding
2. Validation
   a. Founders + Key Strategic Hires
   b. MVP exists
   c. Lighthouse/marquee customers
   d. Seed round funding
3. Growth
   a. Founders + Key Strategic Hires + Engineering Teams
   b. Several customers
   c. A series and beyond

We'll use these generalized stages in the life cycle of a start-up to delineate specific milestones and actions that you should consider taking. So as your start-up and product mature, so does your cybersecurity (Figure I.1).

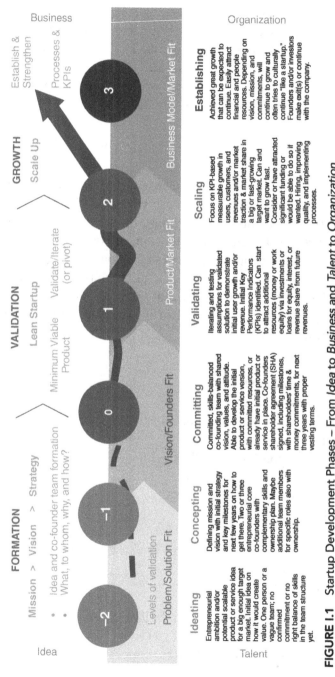

FIGURE I.1 Startup Development Phases – From *Idea* to *Business* and *Talent* to *Organization*

Source: Startup Key Stages by Startup Commons is licensed under a Creative Commons Attribution-ShareAlike 4.0 International License.

PART ONE

Fundamentals

CHAPTER ONE

Minimum Security Investment for Maximum Risk Reduction

An ounce of prevention is worth a pound of cure.

– Benjamin Franklin

N O ONE PLANS ON THEIR START-UP not making it past a year of business, so you should also plan for your investment and planning in cybersecurity to scale into the future. While selecting the bare minimum may seem and feel counterintuitive and is certainly against the opinion of many cybersecurity professionals, it will ensure the continuation of the business.

Just as the heart is the first organ to receive oxygenated blood from the lungs, the continued operation of your start-up should be the number one priority. Security must enable the business to operate and find a balance as a requirement for the business. Cybersecurity is now a priority business function and no longer solely an IT issue.

When discussing cybersecurity many thoughts come to mind, all culminating with three important categories: people, processes, and technology. As a start-up, you won't always have the option of deploying all three. And even many mature organizations do not. This is why when we discuss cybersecurity we must also discuss risk and managing risk. The goal of your cybersecurity strategy should be to reduce, mitigate, and accept risk. No two organizations are the same, even within the same industry vertical. The risk of not being Payment Card Industry Data Security Standard (PCI DSS) certified could mean the loss of revenue for one organization and absolutely nothing to another.

Cybersecurity must be included in your enterprise risk management along with things like compliance, financial reporting, business continuity, etc. It should be all-encompassing and avoid siloing each off into its own risk management vertical. Cybersecurity is a huge part of all of these pieces. All of the following compliance and regulatory requirements require a varying level of cybersecurity practice and maturity (and we'll review these in more detail in Chapter 10):

Payment Card Industry (PCI)
Sarbanes–Oxley Act (SOX)
North American Electric Reliability Corporation (NERC)
Health Insurance Portability and Accountability Act (HIPAA)
HITRUST

The credibility of your business is important to protect. This is why you seek professional advice from lawyers and accountants. A start-up with three founders and without capital cannot afford to hire a full-time world-class lawyer (also referred to as general counsel) or accountant, let alone a chief finance officer (CFO). There are, however, many services that offer those capabilities that can meet a start-up's needs at every phase of the scaling life cycle. You shouldn't feel concerned by the fact that you can't afford a full-time chief information security officer (CISO) or world-class cybersecurity team; alternatives exist that are appropriate for your start-up life cycle stage.

Regardless of the type of business you are starting or industry you plan to sell into, cybersecurity can scale with your idea. From a next-generation weapons system for the military or taking credit card transactions with some new smart device, security can be adequately included. Protecting your intellectual property (IP) and business doesn't require you to have decades of cybersecurity experience; it only requires a willingness and drive to learn. Not everything I discuss will be easy or "point and click," but I will show you the steps along the way to scale your security, along with your business, from seed funding to initial public offering (IPO) or whatever your exit strategy might be.

There is a common phrase when describing old-school cybersecurity approaches where it is like an M&M – crunchy outside and soft inside. When cybersecurity is applied with a hardened perimeter, the thing you want to protect most may actually be more vulnerable from the false sense of security that is created.

When approaching cybersecurity for your new start-up you should focus on the following:

- The data or capabilities you want to protect
- The systems with that data or capabilities you want to protect
- The people with access to those systems you want to protect

COMMUNICATING YOUR CYBERSECURITY

Communication is a critical part of our lives. It is also critical to the success of your business. Communicating with your fellow founders, potential or existing customers, vendors, or investors is vital. In cybersecurity, there is a common philosophy called CIA: confidentiality, integrity, and availability. To better understand this, we can apply this methodology and framework to email. In the case of the sender and intended recipients of that email, only those individuals can access the communications; the information being communicated is unmolested and it is accessible when required respectively. This philosophy is applied across cybersecurity, not just to communicate, but for this discussion we will refer to it as such. It should also be noted that each are not always equal in every situation. There may be times when availability is favored over confidentiality.

You as well as your founders will want to know your start-up is defensible, at a minimum, from the most common threats today. Your customers will want to know their data and, in turn, they are safe with you.

Investors will want to know their investment is not put at unnecessary risk. Once you've addressed the topics we will cover in this book, they will all apply equally to these different audiences. Your message may vary but the standards remain the same.

EMAIL SECURITY

Email has become a digital repository for nearly everything in our lives. From communicating with our children's teachers at school, to our doctors, to our accountant when filing our taxes, it is a literal treasure trove. On top of just the sensitive data in one year of sent and received emails, our email accounts are now the key to accessing nearly all of our other accounts in other systems. Think back to the last time you reset a password. You most likely received a password reset link to your "email address on file."

Email is not secure. This is a bold statement, so let me explain. While you may log in to your email provider that uses HTTPS – S stands for secure – in their web address, when you click to send, that email will be transmitted unencrypted across the Internet. For example, if someone was able to intercept that email when it leaves your email provider's servers they could read the entire contents. For many start-ups, it is not feasible to build and maintain their own email server, so they rely on services like Google Workspace (formally G Suite)[1] or Microsoft O365.

It is important to establish an enterprise-level email account once you register your company domain name. Operating from your personal Gmail, Live, Hotmail, or iCloud email limits the security controls you can place around your account, and does not lend to the credibility of your start-up.

Both Google Workspace and O365[2] are referred to as software-as-a-service (SaaS), which means you don't own any software that you install on your desktop but pay a monthly or yearly service fee. However, there are services such as Virtru[3] that are compatible with those services, both on your desktop and mobile devices, and that allow you to encrypt your emails and control if they can be forwarded and even set an expiration date. This does not prevent someone from copying and pasting the contents or taking a screenshot but would prevent a malicious person from eavesdropping.

For many entrepreneurs, email is not the only means of communication. Surprisingly, many companies operate by text message. Shorter messages that usually get a faster response than lengthy emails can keep start-ups agile but can also pose a risk. Short message system (SMS), also commonly known as text messaging, is insecure like email. You are completely reliant on your cell phone provider's network to provide security of your message. However, when it is transmitted it is unencrypted and you have no confirmation if it has been intercepted or even modified.

I recommend using programs like Signal[4] or Wickr[5] that provide end-to-end encryption, meaning the provider of the service cannot view or even decrypt your message. While too lengthy a topic for this book, this type of messaging is also referred to as zero knowledge encryption, where the service provider has no knowledge of encryption or decryption keys. Some of these providers also have the ability to set an expiration date on messages so they are automatically deleted from the recipient's phone after a specified amount of time. Sometimes, as a start-up, you can't follow every rule of the book to get things going; maybe it is more convenient to quickly share an administrator password to some system and then create a new user. Tools like Signal and Wickr can help you do that quickly and securely.

Chat programs like Slack[6] and Microsoft Teams[7] (included with Microsoft O365) have become hugely popular in large and small businesses alike. It provides an easy-to-use platform to collaborate across teams and physical distances. Like all services, there can be limitations to security based on cost. Some free versions may not allow the same amount of control over data within the platform that you would get if it was paid for.

It is critical to understand the difference between free and paid versions of the same product as well as to read through the terms of service. Most of these platforms encrypt data when it travels over the Internet but may not store it in an encrypted state. The ability to scroll back to the very first message is convenient but also comes at a risk cost of that data being stored somewhere, possibly encrypted. And if that service provider suffers a data breach, it could reveal your chat logs. If it is critical to have total confidentiality and integrity over the messages or data you need to share, then don't use chat platforms.

SECURE YOUR CREDENTIALS

Access to all of these great tools requires nearly the same things: a username and password, at a minimum. Unless you've been living a disconnected lifestyle in the wilderness of Montana, you'll most likely have heard about every major breach in the last 10 years. Of the vendors that respond to these data breaches, one in particular, Verizon, publishes a report[8] every year on the breaches they respond to.

Every year in those reports, the compromise of usernames and passwords are at the top of the list of initial causes of those data breaches. You should treat your usernames and passwords (i.e., credentials) as you would your new amazing start-up intellectual property. Protect them at all costs. Many of the services I discuss in this book provide extra layers of security you can enable called multi-factor authentication (MFA).

The use of MFA is a business requirement today and can drastically reduce, if not eliminate, the possibility of someone that has stolen or guessed your credentials from logging into your account. There are various forms that MFA can come in; a text message is one of the most popular capabilities. However, as we have already discussed, text messages can be insecure.

Multi-factor authentication requires you to enter an additional piece of information when you log in with your credentials. You might even already use a feature like this with your bank where you receive a code via text message that you have to enter to complete the login process. While not all services you use will have this capability, you should enable it immediately, especially if you are like 80% of users that reuse passwords across many sites.

Some more advanced services like Google Workspace for Business allows users to use an app on their phone to conduct the MFA portion of their login. This app is called Google Authenticator and is free to use. Authy[9] and LastPass[10] are also popular free apps. For sites that support this type of MFA, you simply log in to your specific account, enable MFA, and the website provides a QR code that you then take a picture of with the authenticator app.

When using these apps, you will typically be presented with backup codes when you set up this type of multi-factor authentication. Print these

FIGURE 1.1 Yubikey Product Line
Source: https://www.yubico.com

codes out and put them in a secure place. If you lose your phone you lose your ability to authenticate into the services you've protected. I'm saying this twice because it is critical: print out and save your backup codes.

This syncs your phone and the specific account. When you log in with your credentials again you simply open the app and enter the code displayed. There are alternative services to this app, such as Authy. Both of these apps work on iPhone and Android. Large organizations may even employ a physical token that displays a number that changes every

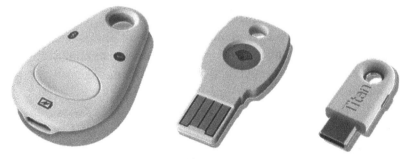

FIGURE 1.2 Google Titan Security Keys
Source: https://cloud.google.com

30 seconds. These physical tokens offer a higher degree of security but are more expensive to deploy and maintain.

SAAS CAN BE SECURE

Nearly gone are the days of setting up a physical server in your garage that runs the website, email, build, dev, staging, and production environments for your start-up. Software-as-a-service (SaaS) allows start-ups to both launch and scale quickly and take advantage of enterprise-level cybersecurity controls. Even in the shared security model adopted by most infrastructure-as-a-service (IaaS) providers like Amazon Web Services (AWS)[11] or Microsoft Azure,[12] a start-up is starting ahead of the game with SaaS.

Starting a business requires a lot of data and documentation and collaboration on that data and documentation. Whether you are developing the next mobile app to disrupt the housing market or developing a new fireproof fabric, the information and intellectual property surrounding that must be secured. Hundreds of platforms exist for collaboration, which I can't discuss at length in this book.

However, I will discuss some of the more popular platforms for sharing data. Some of the most common are Dropbox, Box, Google Drive (part of Google Workspace) and Microsoft OneDrive (part of Microsoft O365). You've probably noticed by now that encryption and access are key components to protecting information. When storing that data you should encrypt it if possible. There are many solutions that have the ability to encrypt files you store in those file-sharing tools and share with your team in an even more secure manner. This doesn't always scale but can help protect your sensitive information early on. Additionally, this level of file-based encryption should be kept for only the most sensitive data to maintain efficiency of your start-up.

In the case of software development, care should be taken when considering access to services such as GitHub,[13] which is a service that allows developers to store and retrieve software code they've written. Ensuring you've enabled all security settings in regard to user access is critical, as you are relying on the service to protect the data once it is on their system. Basics such as making sure you have a strong passphrase set and have enabled multi-factor authentication; making sure your repositories are set to private; and storing things like credentials and keys in a proper secrets manager and not hardcoded in your source code, are essential. Secure development will be discussed further in Chapter 9.

Using SaaS products are not necessarily more secure but they do reduce cost and enable start-ups to remain as lean as possible for as long as possible. Additionally, many of those SaaS platforms will scale with your business, and pricing models adjust accordingly. At some point though, you must use a computer to actually access those services, whether it is a desktop, laptop, or mobile device. For those services to be useful you need availability.

A benefit to using an SaaS platform is a far higher availability rate than if you tried to duplicate the services in your own data center. While the risk can be reduced, you cannot completely outsource risk. If you are negligent with sensitive customer data, like credit card data, you can still be held liable even if you don't host any part of your product in your own data center. This is also referred to as the shared security model.

I've talked about services you might use and the security surrounding them, but you must also consider the security of the devices you use to access them. Desktops, laptops, and mobile devices will continue to be the most likely initial access vector in a data breach along with your credentials. To get your credentials, an attacker must either dupe you into giving your credentials to them, referred to as social engineering, or take advantage of a vulnerability in the computer you are using, referred to as an exploit. Or if you are a high-value target, they may go as far as to gain physical access to your device.

PATCHING

Another primary tenant in cybersecurity is updating and patching; these are critical procedures to achieve balance with confidentiality, integrity, and availability (CIA). That annoying time once a month when you have to close your browser with 50 open tabs or worse, close all your applications, and reboot your computer. The process differs between Windows, MacOS,

Android, and iOS but the goal is the same – a vulnerability is discovered, the vendor creates and releases a patch, and then you must apply the patch.

In the early stages of start-ups, it is a very minimal risk to enable auto-updating in your most-used applications and operating system. This doesn't apply to production environments that are used by paying customers, but we'll get to that in Chapter 9. If you are a typical start-up you will most likely use a laptop and mobile phone. We'll focus on laptops first.

Both Windows and MacOS have the ability to download and install security updates with little interaction required from the user. At most, you will be prompted to reboot your computer, which might take only a few minutes of lost productivity out of your day. However, the security gains from applying those patches immediately will help protect you from devastating ransomware, like WannaCry in 2017, most of the time. Nothing in security is 100%, which is why there are so many layers to a successful cybersecurity program. If you are not sure if this setting is enabled you should check in your system settings in either Windows or MacOS.

Besides monthly updates, there are completely new versions of Windows and Mac released about every 18 months on average. It is not imperative to cybersecurity to immediately spend $200 on the latest version of Windows or Mac if the current version you do use will continue to receive updates. To find out how long you will receive those updates you can search for things like "Windows 10 end of life" or "Mac OS end of life." The results should provide you with the final date on which Microsoft or Apple will discontinue creating security patches. For example, if you are using Windows XP you should immediately buy the latest version of Windows or a new computer, as it is no longer supported by Microsoft and no longer receiving security updates. At the time of writing, the average cost of a ransomware attack on a single system is about $300 to unencrypt your data. Once compromised you can no longer trust the security of that system or the data on that system. In Chapter 7 we'll talk more about what to do if your start-up suffers a data breach.

The next layer of security you must be aware of is the applications you might use on a daily basis: Chrome, Firefox, Safari, Office, Slack, etc. All the components you use to create and run your start-up, these too can be vulnerable. I mentioned earlier that stolen credentials are one of the leading causes of data breaches. And those credentials are typically stolen in one of two ways: social engineering or software vulnerability exploitation.

Example 1

For example, you get an email from a prospective venture capital company looking to participate in your Series A funding round. The email has an attachment with their terms; you open it. This email plays on human emotion and counts on you dropping your guard and best interest for your company to open the attachment. Suddenly you get a popup that says the contents of your computer have been encrypted. You've been hit with ransomware.

Example 2

You receive a phone call from an individual at a venture capital firm you've been speaking with about participating in your next round. They tell you they're sending an email with a link to their secure portal to access the terms sheet. You get an email a few minutes after you hang up the call, click the link, it prompts you to log in with your Microsoft O365 credentials. Once logged in you try to open the document and get an error. You call the number back and get a message saying the number is not in service. Suddenly you get a frantic text from your co-founder that production is down hard. You've fallen victim to pre-texting and credential compromise. Since your credentials also worked in your cloud provider account the attackers were able to ransom all of the data in your production database.

In these scenarios, both social engineering and vulnerability exploitation came into play. The email enticed you to open it and then open the attachment. The attachment then contained an exploit that gained special privileges on your computer and encrypted all of your data. The phone call made the email you received shortly after seem more legitimate. While there is no software update that can prevent you from opening the email and attachment, you could possibly prevent the opened document from harming your computer.

All of the five applications I mentioned receive frequent security updates, some more than others. These are just as important to apply as the ones for Windows or MacOS. Some applications will have the ability to automatically download and install updates, but most will not. This will require a small amount of effort on your part to make sure your most used

(continued)

(continued)

applications are up to date. I recommend checking updates for your web browser, like Chrome, Firefox, and Safari, and any productivity applications, like Word, Excel or PowerPoint. And if you use an email client on your computers, like Outlook or Thunderbird. These types of applications should be updated as quickly as possible; vulnerabilities are constantly discovered since they are the easiest way to compromise a system.

ANTIVIRUS IS STILL NECESSARY BUT GOES BY A DIFFERENT NAME

You might be thinking, "Well, what about antivirus?" I've devoted all of Chapter 4 to this topic because of the volume and complexity of solutions available. I also discuss many options that may require capital expenditure that might not seem so lean for a start-up. Just know if you happen to use pirated software you will not be able to receive critical security updates. You also cannot verify the authenticity of what you've downloaded and could very well have opened a backdoor into your system for attackers. Legitimate start-ups should only use legitimate software.

Open source software, which is a legitimate free option, can also come with risks. Depending on the country your start-up is founded in, you may need to pay close attention to open source software from specific countries and geographic locations. This applies to antivirus software or anything else you use in your start-up.

So, what do they call antivirus these days? Marketing has now rebranded this technology as endpoint detection and response (EDR). While it does have many more features than the popular antivirus software of the 90s and 00s, it still has basically the same functions and keeps your device secure. We'll dive into this more in Chapter 4.

MOBILE DEVICES

Mobile devices are now woven into the fabric of everyday business – smartphones, tablets, etc., are used to run and secure your start-up.

These have the same level of access to critical information as your laptop. Many MFA solutions, which I discussed earlier, run as apps on your smartphone; physical tokens are still the most secure but not as convenient as a mobile app. Our mobile devices are now acting as the keys to the digital kingdom. Nearly all the same security rules we've discussed so far apply to our mobile phones and devices. You must make sure the operating system is up to date; keep installed applications up to date; set a strong passcode, fingerprint authentication, or face authentication; and encrypt the phone if it is not on by default for your make and model. Some of this is not already activated out of the box and is easy to skip over in the setup process.

Setting a passcode, passphrase, pattern, or fingerprint is the first line of defense to protecting the data on your phone and the data it has access to. Nearly all modern devices support these features and you should enable them when you buy the phone or do so immediately. There are many lines of thought on which option is most secure, again a larger discussion than can be covered in this book, but you should enable at least one of them. You should also encrypt your phone in the case that it is lost or stolen. While most thieves resell the phones and don't attempt to retrieve data from them, encrypting your phone will provide peace of mind if it goes missing. Both Google and Apple offer the capability to find your phone if it is lost, or remotely delete all sensitive data if it is stolen. These features are not enabled by default and you should ensure you switch them on for any device you use for conducting business.

When a device is lost or stolen you have now lost your ability to log in to services that require your MFA code, such as Google Workspace or Apple iCloud. Both services have procedures that will allow you to log in after an emergency but it can be a lengthy process. Both services do allow you to set up an emergency phone. This should be someone you trust explicitly: a co-founder, spouse, or another family member whose device you could quickly access in an emergency. So preferably not someone that lives on a different continent. Or you could even have a second phone that you leave locked away for such an event, depending on how critical your data is.

As you scale, it becomes more important to manage these devices. This will certainly be a business decision that is made on whether to issue mobile devices to employees. This provides stronger controls around how users access your sensitive data, but also requires employees to now carry two devices. Another option is to require employees to install corporate mobile device management software on their phone to block certain apps from accessing your data. Or to force users to use only certain applications to access your start-up's sensitive data. This option requires careful consideration based on local, state, and federal laws not only where your start-up is located but also where your employees are located. There can be privacy implications as well as employees refusing to give access to their personal device.

 ## SUMMARY

Regardless of the stage of your company – formation, validation, or growth – these are all unique starting points and require a different effort and level of investment of resources. Understanding the foundational components will help you determine where you must start or where you need to accelerate projects. Not everyone bakes in cybersecurity from the day they sign the documents to legally form their business.

Identify the stage your company is at and then build your cybersecurity program to at least that level. Make sure you identify the risks that may have been overlooked in previous stages of the company. Both technical debt and cybersecurity debt are a real thing. The longer you put it off, the more that debt scales with your business.

 ## ACTION PLAN

- Determine what stage your business is at: formation, validation, or growth.
- Define and write down who your ideal customers are.
- Write down what industries they are in.
- Write down what data, if any, you will process, store, access, or in any way have access to.

NOTES

1. https://workspace.google.com/
2. https://www.office.com/
3. https://www.virtru.com/
4. https://signal.org/
5. https://wickr.com/
6. https://slack.com/
7. https://www.microsoft.com/en-ca/microsoft-365/microsoft-teams/group-chat-software
8. https://enterprise.verizon.com/resources/reports/dbir/
9. https://authy.com/
10. https://www.lastpass.com/
11. https://aws.amazon.com/
12. https://azure.microsoft.com/en-us/
13. https://github.com/

CHAPTER TWO

Cybersecurity Strategy and Roadmap Development

Proper Planning and Preparation Prevents Piss Poor Performance

– Military Adage

A CYBERSECURITY STRATEGY AND ROADMAP may look very barren for a start-up that is pre-seed investment. If your product does not yet exist outside of a great idea, it might seem there is little to plan for at the moment. This is a misconception and you can and should plan for cybersecurity to be part of your business and culture from the beginning. Your cybersecurity strategy should be developed shortly after creating your business plan and defining what your business is. This information will define how and where you apply cybersecurity.

Questions you must answer:

- What type of business is this?
- What types of customers will we sell to?
- What types of information will the business consume?

- What types of information will the business create?
- Where will this business be conducted?

 ## WHAT TYPE OF BUSINESS IS THIS?

The type of business is important, to understand how cybersecurity will scale with the company. If you are developing a free-to-download Android and iOS game with in-game purchases, your application of cybersecurity might progress slower than a biotech start-up developing a new drug to treat a rare disease.

In one case, the mobile game company would most likely survive if the first beta version of source code was stolen. In another, a biotech pharmaceutical might not survive if all R&D information was stolen by a nation-state and given to a foreign competitor. A company that loses control of credit card numbers may suffer limited damage, but one that loses control of social security numbers may not. Credit card numbers can be replaced; a social security number cannot.

However, when you consider the prevalence and increasing severity of ransomware cases, this threat could close any of these companies for good.

Defining your business will help to answer all other questions and allow you to build your strategy and roadmap that will scale with your business.

 ## WHAT TYPES OF CUSTOMERS WILL WE SELL TO?

Once you know what type of company you are building, it should be relatively easy to identify who your customers are. Business-to-business (B2B) and business-to-consumer (B2C) are very different organizations that will require different tooling of your strategy. If you are developing a mobile app for 18- to-24-year-olds you will most likely never receive a third-party vendor assessment from a risk management team to evaluate the maturity and efficacy of your cybersecurity and how you securely manage their data.

However, if the company's main purpose is to sell into the mobile provider market you will most likely have completely separate cybersecurity addendums attached to contracts in order to do business with those firms. When you identify who you are selling to you will be able to better understand and anticipate cybersecurity requirements and how mature your program must be.

- Are the customers businesses or individuals?
- Where are the customers geographically located?
- What industries are the customers in?

WHAT TYPES OF INFORMATION WILL THE BUSINESS CONSUME?

You must also think of the data your company will take in. This could be data from your customers, business partners, users, and even employees. Much of what we discuss in Chapter 9 and Chapter 10 will be applicable here and create requirements and liabilities. This is also a good gut check of "do we really need this data?" It is hard to predict the future needs of said data, but it is very easy to calculate the fines associated with exposing the personal data of 100,000 of your beta users.

The Ponemon Institute, in conjunction with IBM, calculated a cost of $242 in the US for each record exposed in a data breach.[1]

WHAT TYPES OF INFORMATION WILL THE BUSINESS CREATE?

Will your start-up be creating proprietary data as part of the product you are building? Naturally, every business creates proprietary data in the course of day-to-day business. But if you are taking seemingly disparate data sources and combining them into a new type of credit risk for banks to use, that could be very sensitive data, requiring a much higher level of protection than the data source parts.

When considering the data your start-up will deal with, it is also important to understand the engineering requirements. Many of the regulations and laws discussed in Chapter 11 require anonymization or deidentification of data. This is something worth getting right at the start. If the system is designed to ensure data can be deidentified and still be valuable to the business you can reduce both cybersecurity and privacy risks.

WHERE GEOGRAPHICALLY WILL BUSINESS BE CONDUCTED?

Where your business is headquartered and the locations you plan to conduct business and have customers will influence how much or how little cybersecurity you will need at each phase from formation, to validation, to growth. We scratch the surface for laws and regulations in Chapter 10. For example, if you will have any data from European Union citizens, then you will have to comply with GDPR, regardless of the phase you are in.

BUILDING THE ROADMAP

This document can be really any form or format that you choose. There is no rule that it should be in Word or Google Doc or slides or even highly detailed charts in a spreadsheet. At a minimum I would suggest started with a text document where you can expand an extrapolate on thoughts. Once you feel that document captures your roadmap, then you could look at extracting what you've written into slides or charts.

The roadmap can be solely an internally document. This does not need to be shared with investors, your board or customers. If you plan to be aggressive and forward leaning in how your start-up approaches cybersecurity, you could certainly build the document to be shareable from the start. Much of what you write in this document could later be used for cybersecurity certifications, so this is valuable work to do.

Opening Statement

An opening statement or overview should contain your thoughts and vision for cybersecurity in your organization. Answering questions for the reader such as why cybersecurity is even important to your start-up, why you are making it a goal for the company and why make the capital investment in it. What exactly are you trying to secure or ensure the security of? This will set the tone for the document and whoever the intended audience will be.

You could also talk to the scope of the roadmap. Is cybersecurity purely product focused or will it also ensure the security and safety of your offices?

Stakeholders

Describe who is part of this roadmap. What parts of the business and who is responsible and also who is interested? Your founding team will most likely be responsible and your board and customers most likely would be interested parties.

Tactics

What will be the actions of this plan and what is the timeline? Typically, a roadmap might lay out a plan for 12 to 36 months, some may even opt to look as far as 5 years. As you read through this book and understand the specific tactical components and actions you need to take to start-up secure you will have greater understanding of what your start-up needs in its roadmap. There is an important distinction to point out that what needs to be in the roadmap and what should be in the roadmap are two different things. Needs are immediate and foundational. Items you should have are long term and require other parts and pieces to come into place. You need strong passphrases and should have certifications like SOC2. However, you must address many needs before addressing SOC2.

Measurability

At a minimum you should have a way to measure the success of this roadmap. Whether that is through OKRs, KPIs or other metrics methodology you and your founding team use, a way to define success is critical to the success of this roadmap. Without a way to measure it this document will simply be a document that gathers dust.

Stating how it will be measured and with what frequency informs the intended audience that this is a guiding business document intended to steer business decisions going forward.

▮ CASE STUDY

Monique and Jack are veterans of the fashion and tech industry. They were inspired to build a start-up after seeing a market gap between high-end fashion accessories, and buyers that were out of reach. They are now one year in and have raised angel and seed funding to build their high-end fashion accessory rental business. With both a web front-end and mobile app they've passed $150,000 in monthly reoccurring revenue (MRR) with their lean team of 37 full-time employees.

Having both worked in the tech industry, they understand the need for cybersecurity but don't know where to start. Monique gets a Twitter notification from a popular tech industry news website that a competitor of theirs, who is the current leader in the space and plans to IPO (initial public offering) in the coming months, has suffered a material ransomware attack. Monique texts the story to Jack and calls for an urgent executive staff meeting to discuss their risks.

Monique and Jack don't have a chief information security officer (CISO) yet, or even cybersecurity engineers. Sarah, their chief technology officer (CTO) and first executive hire, has strong software and cloud engineering experience but only a general understanding of cybersecurity. The executive team decides to work the problem backward from being attacked by ransomware to the steps they need to take to defend against it in the first place.

Jack contacts key board members and advisors to identify firms and possible new advisors that can provide technical cybersecurity guidance. The executive team formulates a list of their customers and the data they have on them. Michael, their chief marketing officer (CMO), mentions a planned advertising campaign in English-speaking European Union (EU) countries to expand users internationally. The team almost simultaneously realizes they have not considered GDPR or hired a data privacy officer (DPO) in the EU.

During further discussions of how a similar ransomware attack would affect them, Sarah mentions that while most of the platform is hosted in a single cloud provider, they are using a different provider for backup. Now they have two locations for customer data.

After a couple hours of discussion, the team has answered many key questions of how ransomware would impact their business:

- Who are our customers?
- What data do we have on our customers, including personal data?
- Where do we store the data we have on our customers?
- Who would we call if we suffered a ransomware attack?
- Do we have any controls in place to defend against the example that affected our competitor?
- How long could we survive the attack and how long can our product be down for?
- How long would it take to recover fully from the attack?
- How would we notify customers, the board, investors, and the general public?
- Which executive is responsible for each of these questions?

They have also received recommendations from board members on cybersecurity firms to assist in a technical cybersecurity assessment of their environment. Lastly, they have decided to maintain their current burn rate for at least another 8 months before considering building in-house cybersecurity expertise and focus on external cost-effective advisors and firms. The team now has a rough plan of action and roadmap for this very specific threat and an overall plan of how to start addressing cybersecurity risks in general as a business.

- Monique will contact their outside counsel and, together with their CMO, will find an EU law firm to act as their DPO.
- Sarah and Jack will finalize a list of data types they store for personal data of customers and where that data is located.
- Sarah will define a scope for the recommended cybersecurity firm to assess their cybersecurity controls around production and customer data.
- Sarah and Jack will own driving the resolution of any findings from that assessment and report back to the executive team with an 18-month cybersecurity roadmap.

- Monique will contact their insurance broker to verify that they are covered for ransomware and to get additional advice for the business on steps to take if they are attacked.
- Monique and the CMO will work with outside counsel to develop boilerplate notification language to send to customers in the event they are attacked.

 ## SUMMARY

Your cybersecurity strategy and roadmap will be living documents. Be prepared to change them as the environment around your start-up changes, and as your start-up itself changes. These documents and plans are a guide and shouldn't be a rigid rule that you develop in January and must still follow 11 months later in November when the environment is drastically different.

Answer the questions we talked about in this chapter to understand your start-up's overall risks and how those will drive compliance, regulatory, legal, and other requirements to become and remain secure. You are always secure until the data breach happens, which we talk about in Chapter 12.

 ## ACTION PLAN

- Write down the answers to the questions in this chapter.
- Based on those answers go to Chapters 9 and 10 and write down what you may need to comply with.
- Reference those controls against what you may already have put in place from Chapters 3 through 6.

 ## NOTE

1. https://www.ibm.com/security/data-breach

CHAPTER THREE

Secure Your Credentials

I changed my password everywhere to
"incorrect." That way when I forget it, it always
reminds me, "Your password is incorrect."

– Anonymous

J UST BECAUSE YOU ARE A START-UP does not mean you are not a target. Before you have an amazing product that your unicorn start-up has built you have to log in to something. Your credentials, for everything, are a critical key to starting secure and remaining secure. Whether you are logging into your phone, laptop, email, chat app, or cloud environment, the first step is your username and password.

If you only read one chapter in this book, this is the one. Verizon publishes an annual report called the Data Breach and Investigations Report (DBIR), pronounced "deebur." This report details thousands of data breach cases that Verizon analyzes and investigates in real-world examples. And every year user credentials are part of the top list of vectors that attackers use to gain access to systems and sensitive data at thousands of companies, large and small, around the world.

PASSWORD MANAGERS

Password Managers are software-as-a-service (SaaS) tools that allow you to securely store and manage many sets of unique credentials across websites and all manner of systems where you use a combination of username and passphrase to access. Some solutions even offer non-cloud-based products; this is a bit riskier, since it is stored on your device and if, for some reason, you lose access to that device, you could lose all your credentials.

There are many great options for these solutions. For example (in no particular order):

LastPass[1]
Dashlane[2]
1Password[3]

These are some of the more popular password manager solutions available and offer many great features. These all have browser extensions that let you automatically fill in the username and password so you never have to open the solutions directly and copy and paste the information.

This can have a very useful side effect of helping protect you from some phishing that tries to harvest your credentials. Maybe you get a very convincing email, click the link and are presented with a login screen for your Office 365 (O365) account. A password manager will see the domain does not match the real one and won't enter your username and password automatically. In addition, some of these have desktop apps that add additional functionality and most have mobile apps to bring that same functionality and security to the apps on your phone.

Setting up a password manager is pretty straightforward, and they all do a great job of teaching how to use the tool. When you first set up your password manager, this is where it is critical to have another passphrase to remember. You should never reuse passphrases, so the passphrase for your password manager should be different from the passphrase you use for your laptop or anywhere else.

Pay close attention to selecting these tools' enterprise capabilities. As your company grows through formation, validation, and growth, you may outgrow some of these solutions. Most will work for personal use but not all password managers scale up to a large corporate environment with hundreds or thousands of users.

Scaling questions you should ask:

- Does it support Oauth?[4]
- Does it support OpenID?[5]
- Does it support Single Sign-on?
- Will it integrate with directory solutions like Microsoft Active Directory or Google Workspace?
- Are there administrative roles for IT and cybersecurity teams?

Under no circumstances should you use the passphrase for your password manager anywhere else! I want to repeat this since it is so important to the security of your new password manager. Finally, all of the solutions I mentioned support multi-factor authentication. Multi-factor authentication can come in many forms, which we'll discuss later in this chapter.

PASSPHRASE

You most likely have already heard "create a strong and complex password" if you've ever worked at any company that uses computers. So we already know what we should be doing. But this gets to be completely impossible when there are hundreds of sites and systems you might log into in a single day. In reality you should only have to remember two or three passwords. One for your computer, one for your password manager (which we will talk about next), and maybe another for some other unique system. Let's start with your device.

You will most likely be starting with your personal devices as a start-up. You probably won't be using Microsoft Active Directory or some SaaS directory service to manage identities just yet, maybe never. So the best way to protect logging into your device is with a long passphrase.

A passphrase is something that is very easy for you to remember. It does not need to have a capital letter for each word, lower case letter, number, or even a special character. However, depending on the system you set this passphrase in, you might be forced to use a combination of uppercase, lowercase, numbers, and special characters. It just needs to be as long as you can make it. This is called entropy.

If you haven't been living under a rock, you've most likely seen the news over the years of data breach after data breach. Millions of user records are compromised and stolen each year. Many of these result in users' passwords being exposed, and many of these passwords are 12 characters or less! So the longer your passphrase the better. There is a very useful website run by a prominent security researcher called haveibeenpwnd.com. Here you can enter your email address and check to see if it has ever appeared in a known data breach. This typically indicates whether your password associated with that account was compromised in any data breach.

Creating a passphrase is pretty simple: think of a sentence that you can always remember. It's as simple as that. Remember: the longer the better. Since most systems still require different character types, be sure to use uppercase, lowercase, and punctuation to meet those system requirements in the meantime. If you pick a phrase from a favorite book or something common, change it a little, replace a word with one that doesn't make sense, get creative.

Obviously opening our laptop isn't the only time we will log in. We have email, social media, chat apps, and hundreds of other places we need to access to get our start-up off the ground and keep it going. The only option to keep these as secure as possible from the start is using a different password with every single account.

This would be impossible to remember. Which brings us back to password managers. These incredibly useful tools have gained popularity in the last decade as we've realized password reuse is extremely insecure. When an attacker figures out your password, then they can log in to every other account you might have. So having the same password for your email account and root Amazon Web Service (AWS) account can have devastating consequences.

We mentioned at the start of this chapter the Verizon DBIR that is published every year that illustrates how usernames and passwords are a significant part of breaches. Many services ask you to use your email as a username. So once your email and your reused password are compromised, attackers will try that combination across every site you might use. This is why having unique passwords for every account is so critical. The following diagram depicts the typically user experience when using multi-factor authentication.

FIGURE 3.1   Example of a Push-Based MFA
Source: https://www.sectorlink.com/article/what-is-multi-factor-authentication

MULTI-FACTOR AUTHENTICATION

Multi-factor authentication (MFA), sometimes called second factor authentication (2FA), is another component to the login process for any system. You've most likely come across a variant of this with your bank and received an SMS text with a six or eight digit one-time use code needed when you log in, used in addition to your username and passphrase. Another popular option is push-based MFA where you receive a notification on your mobile device to either approve or deny access with one-touch. Figure 3.1 shows the typical user experience of this type of MFA.

There are many options here and unfortunately the cybersecurity industry has done you and all users a disservice with making it unnecessarily complicated. I'll do my best to undo that here. We already mentioned SMS, which is one option; let's start with the strongest option and work our way back to SMS.

We discussed physical tokens briefly in the first chapter. This is by far the most secure multi-factor authentication option currently available. One of the original vendors in this space was RSA. They produce a small device with an LCD screen that displays a six-digit code that changes every 30 seconds. This code is what you then use in conjunction with your username and password to log in to some system. The downside is that you would typically have a corresponding physical server, which the token is synced with before it is given to a user. Obviously, this deployment model does not work for a small start-up or even a 500-person start-up for that matter. It does have its uses in such situations where you are not allowed to bring a phone or USB device, such as classified environments.

These devices were rarely used, only seen in large corporate environments, and typically used for logging into a corporate virtual private network (VPN). They were not at all user friendly and not accessible to consumers, due to the requirement of a physical server hosted in your corporate data center that the token was synced to before being issued to the user. These systems are also vulnerable to the rare occurrence where the tokens become out of sync with the server and users are no longer able to authenticate.

Luckily, the cybersecurity industry has nearly democratized multi-factor authentication and as a founder you now have options, such as YubiKey[6] or Google Titan.[7] These are small physical tokens that you can either plug in to a system and tap a small metal disc to authenticate, or simply press the device against your phone to authenticate through a wireless technology standard called near field communication (NFC). These devices are widely supported, and more systems and services support them every day through another technology standard called Fast ID Online (FIDO).[8] These devices are also economical compared to the value they provide and range anywhere from $20 to $50.

There are now also many other mobile apps that act as a soft token. These soft tokens, which also generate a series of random numbers of four to eight in length, are apps you download from the Google Play or Apple App Store. There are several apps to choose from, such as Authy, Google Authenticator, LastPass (they also make a password manager), Duo, and several others. These are typically easy to use and set up. When turning on multi-factor authentication in a service or system that supports this type of MFA you will typically be presented with a QR code on your screen. When you add a new account in the MFA app of your choosing it will ask you to point your camera at the screen, which reads the QR code and syncs that account with your phone. Most of these apps are free. The cost comes in when you want more enterprise features and the ability to manage many users. You should carefully review an app's features before committing. Some apps do not allow you to back up your soft token so you can easily move to a new device or phone when you upgrade. One can make the argument both for and against this capability. On one hand it can open a vulnerability of backing up those codes and then restoring them on another device. On the other, the convenience may outweigh the

integrity. This entails another balancing act with confidentiality, integrity, and availability (the CIA triad).

Finally, SMS text messages are a valid form of multi-factor authentication; they may not be ideal or the most secure, but are better than nothing. With SMS-based multi-factor authentication you are sent a text message with a unique code to your mobile phone number, which you then use along with your username and password, just like the previous options we discussed. SMS has been shown to be vulnerable to various attacks due to the underlying telephone network protocols. There are several infamous Twitter account takeovers that occurred because of vulnerabilities in SMS. These attacks used a combination of social engineering to get the mobile provider to conduct a port of the victim's phone number to a new SIM. Once complete, the attacker was then able to receive all phone calls and messages for the victim's mobile phone number because it was associated with the attacker's SIM in their mobile device. Even if SMS is the only option, enable it as a minimum. And if SMS is truly the only option, you should also call your mobile provider and add additional security to your account. Many providers today are aware of this attack and allow you to set up a separate phone password when calling in to access your account. Some also will put a port lock on your account, which requires you to physically visit a store to port your number. It only takes a few minutes on the phone to enable these controls that can save hours or days of heartache.

ENTITLEMENTS

With every system you have access to, you will have some level of entitlements. This is sometimes referred to as your role and rights within that system. You can think of this as the difference between a user account and an administrator account, which both have different entitlements in the system. These determine what you are able to do within that system.

Keeping track of this when it is yourself and one or two other founders is pretty easy. You might only have a few systems to access, and a few SaaS applications to log in to, but don't be fooled into taking the easy route here. Many start-ups get sucked into the mantra of "we'll fix it later" or "we'll set up better controls when we scale" – this thinking is setting you up for failure.

While it might seem easier to just give everyone administrative rights to their laptop, cloud workloads, and your sales CRM system, this becomes very difficult to undo in the future. And you don't want to make this discovery during an audit for a vital security certification for your start-up.

A common trap start-ups fall into when setting up their minimally viable product (MVP) is that they build systems in the fastest and easiest way possible. This sometimes does not account for near- and long-term future requirements. A great example is the mixing of user accounts and service accounts. A user account, simply put, is an account in a system, any system, used by a carbon-based life form. A service account is an account used by a system, application, or anything that is not a human.

While this does not seem like a huge deal right now, if the small amount of time is not put in to design and build your system for the future and to scale, the cost in the future will be exponential. Businesses are risky and complex, just as complex as human relationships. If you are in the formation phase building your product and a few years later a founder leaves for whatever reason, it could spell disaster.

When systems are built on top of user accounts, and when that user account is suddenly disabled or terminated, it could bring your entire production environment to a grinding halt. I've personally seen it happen at what would be considered very mature companies. And if you want to stay compliant with your security certifications, you can't simply turn a user's account back on for someone who no longer works at the company.

If you are moving from formation to validation, take an extremely close look at how your product is architected. Eliminate any user accounts that are being used as service accounts. If you are in growth stage and beyond, you should have absolutely no user accounts being used as a service account.

KEY MANAGEMENT

There are many different types of keys a start-up will need to protect, even from the very start. We are not talking about physical metal keys on your keychain but digital keys to your systems. Regardless of the type of key, these should be protected just as much as you would your passphrases. You may have secure shell (SSH) keys used to access a system. Or, if you are building an SaaS application, you might have application programming interface (API) keys. And if you are dealing with sensitive data, your start-up may need to manage encryption keys.

There are many other types of digital keys, but those we just mentioned are some of the more common ones. When it comes to SSH keys it is best practice to secure the private key with a strong passphrase when generating your public and private key. As you scale you should absolutely implement an SSH key management solution. This will help you manage many keys in your environment and keep an accurate accounting of the keys. Always make sure keys are never shared; a key should only be used and associated with one individual. Make sure to remove unneeded keys; this will be complex and error prone as you scale if you have not implemented a key management solution. Finally, never hardcode an SSH key, or any key for that matter, into code.

Application programing interface (API) keys are used typically to allow two systems to programmatically authenticate and exchange data. These keys should be treated in more or less the same way as your SSH keys. Never hardcode API keys into your application. This can expose the key to potential attackers and provide access to your application or systems. Store API keys in a key management system, never in your code repository. Always limit scope and access to API keys, and avoid creating API keys with unlimited access when at all possible. It might be convenient to create one API key that can access everything you might need; however, this can create significant risk to data in that system.

We'll discuss keys more in Chapter 6, "Your Product in the Cloud."

CASE STUDY

After graduating with a degree in computer science and agriculture, respectively, Ali and Rebecca – who met while interning at the same agri-tech company – decided to found their own start-up. During their internship they saw inefficiencies in farming in underdeveloped nations that could benefit from applying machine learning to traditional farming techniques. After winning $750,000 in seed funding from an accelerator, they passed $150MM in annual reoccurring revenue (ARR) three years later, with over 1700 customers.

During the most recent board meeting, a board member asked how the business was protecting its intellectual property after reading a report about specific nation-states targeting their sector. Ali and Rebecca responded with their results from the pre-IPO assessment that was conducted 6 months prior, which found only minor gaps in processes. Ali committed to the board by the next meeting that they would conduct an in-depth cybersecurity maturity assessment of the product, which included cloud-connected, smart farming devices over 5G and satellite networks.

Ali and Rebecca have been excellent stewards of the capital invested in the company and have only grown to 189 full-time employees and out-source all manufacturing of their cloud-connected farm equipment. However, the cybersecurity assessment found significant gaps in how access to data and systems was protected.

Ali, Rebecca, their CTO, and Chief Data Scientist all still had root access to their cloud infrastructure through a single shared account. Additionally, developers were storing API keys in code and in plain text files on their laptops. Finally, developers were also using shared credentials for all cloud systems, even between dev, staging, and production, without multi-factor authentication. Ali and Rebecca knew about all of this, since they were key to developing the product they are selling, and those habits were passed to new hires. However, they did not realize the extent of the risk until it was documented as critical findings in the assessment report.

The report recommended several actions:

- Remove all shared accounts and provide each individual with a unique account.
- Remove unneeded access from privileged users.
- Roll all API keys, because they've been embedded in code for the life of the start-up.
- Implement a password manager.
- Force multi-factor authentication on all cloud infrastructure.
- Implement a secrets manager.

Removing executives' root access to the cloud infrastructure was easy and painless. They were easily able to set up a single root account where the password was split into two halves. One half was known by one senior DevOps engineer and the other half by the director of DevOps. Buying and implementing a password manager was also relatively straightforward after their CTO examined several different vendors for the requirements they developed. Implementing a secrets manager took many months, as automated deployment tooling was already set up for the old way of working and now had to be redesigned from the ground up. They were able to solve multi-factor authentication by using their current identity provider, who already supported that feature and was a single-setting change.

Rolling the API keys was a different story. After one month of planning, the DevOps team began to roll these API keys. Because there was no documentation on exactly what keys went to what customer system, they experienced several self-inflicted outages resulting in $872,900 in SLA credits to those customers. There was also another 1700 people-hours' worth of development work required to change code that initially relied on hard-coded API keys to now use functionality in the secrets management system. They also lost a customer renewal after the required firmware upgrade, due to all the infrastructure changes having failed, completely bricking a customer's equipment.

The lessons learned and presented in the next board meeting found that if they had implemented relatively inexpensive tooling earlier on in the development of the product, these issues would have been avoided.

SUMMARY

In my opinion, this is the most important chapter in this book. Access to a system is the single greatest linchpin in the security of a system. Using strong passphrases, not passwords, that are also unique for each system is a must. Making it easy to do this requires that you use a password manager. Remember, the free password manager in your browser that is included with your operating system will most likely not scale with your start-up. If you keep a free option, make sure they do have enterprise tiers.

Finally, adding multi-factor authentication to those critical accounts, preferably with a physical token like Yubikey or Google Titan, will ensure the highest level of security. These are inexpensive and provide considerable value far beyond their typical $30 price tag.

 ACTION PLAN

- Go create a strong passphrase and set it on your laptop.
- Purchase a physical multi-factor authentication token.
- Sign up for a password manager:
    - Set a strong passphrase, different than any others you are using.
    - Set up hardware-based multi-factor authentication.
    - Get all of your accounts loaded in it.
- Set up a soft, multi-factor authentication token app on your phone.
- Set your most critical accounts to the highest possible security settings and enable multi-factor authentication on all of them.
- Go back to Chapter 2 and the roadmap document you've started and add any needed roadmap items.

 NOTES

1. https://www.lastpass.com/
2. https://www.dashlane.com/
3. https://1password.com/
4. https://oauth.net/
5. https://openid.net/
6. https://www.yubico.com/
7. https://cloud.google.com/titan-security-key
8. https://fidoalliance.org/

CHAPTER FOUR

Endpoint Protection

The quieter you become, the more you hear.

– Ram Dass

YOUR LAPTOP, DESKTOP, CLOUD ENVIRONMENT, smartphone, and tablet are integral parts to running a successful business. Checking email and social media, getting on conference calls with prospective clients and investors, and presenting your business plan to investors are just some of the critical tasks we use these devices for.

For any start-up, or even a one-hundred-year-old business, these pieces of technology are a requirement, not an option. Clients, investors, and vendors expect a prompt reply to an email or returned phone call for voicemail. The success of your business can hinge on a $200 smartphone and $80-per-month business Internet connection with Wi-Fi.

It is crucial to protect these devices as well as the data on them and the data they have access to. Threats today are well beyond the scope of traditional antivirus we all know well, like the Symantecs of the world. Antivirus as we know it has for the past 20 years been primarily based on simple pattern matching and heuristic analysis that could detect new

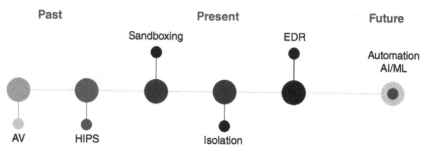

FIGURE 4.1 Diagram Showing the Progression of Endpoint Security
Source: https://www.criticalstart.com/endpoint-solutions-epp-vs-edr-vs-mdr/

viruses that may use similar components of software code as other viruses. This worked very well for years; however, the threats of today are far more advanced, skilled, and capable. These methods fall short to even protect against common ransomware. Figure 4.1 shows where endpoint security started several decades ago and where it is today.[1,2]

■ VENDORS

The antivirus industry has moved away from using the term "antivirus" in their products to terminology such as endpoint protection platform (EPP) and endpoint detection and response (EDR). These new software security products provide incredibly advanced features to stop breaches before they occur and greatly aid in the investigation of a breach when it is not prevented.

There are numerous vendors in this space and many support desktops and smart devices. While it is always beneficial to use the same vendor across devices, it is not essential. Selecting a product can be complex but there are several solutions I recommend. These are based on their support for multiple types of systems: Windows, Linux, Mac, Android, and iOS. Some vendors include:

- CrowdStrike[3]
- Carbon Black[4] (now owned by VMware)
- Cylance[5] (now owned by BlackBerry)
- SentinalOne[6]

- Microsoft[7]
- FireEye[8]
- Trend Micro[9]
- Capsule8[10]
- LimaCharlie[11]

This by no means is an exhaustive list.

There are currently several open source or free commercial EDR solutions on the market. However, for running a lean start-up there are several options that come very close. You should also keep in mind that "free" doesn't always mean free. Some products may come with ads to upsell or provide an extensive amount of useful information back to the vendor. You should closely review the terms and conditions of the product you select with your general counsel. Some vendors include:

- Wazuh[12]
- BLUESPAWN[13]
- Comodo EDR[14]

SELECTING AN EDR

There are trade-offs to not having to pay an annual subscription. If running lean is a priority, I wouldn't get discouraged by these trade-offs. You should, however, consider and understand the risks, based on your business. While the likelihood of an attacker gaining access to your environment through a security vendor is low, it should be accounted for. If you have proprietary data that, once lost, a competitor could duplicate or emulate your product very closely, it should be adequately protected.

Running consumer-level EPP is adequate and reasonable up until

- you've raised and closed a seed round, or
- you have over 45 employees, or
- you are processing or storing sensitive data.

The easiest first step is to determine if the product supports your operating systems. Every vendor supports Windows, many support Apple MacOS, and some even support Linux. This is important because as your start-up scales you may find your technology begins to become more diverse and the product you select will need to support those new systems.

There is great benefit to using the same solution across all systems, but this might not always be possible. Some vendors are leaders in capabilities on Windows or MacOS or Linux. You must consider many things like cost, ease of use, and ease of manageability when deciding to use more than one vendor.

Many of the paid vendors offer managed services. This can be ideal for a start-up that is not yet ready or at the appropriate stage to hire their first cybersecurity professional. There is, of course, a cost associated with this, but it is typically far less than hiring an individual to manage the product.

Open source solutions will obviously require more effort on your part to both deploy and maintain, and they are not designed for your average end user. Again, there are other vendors that offer services to manage these free products for you. While there are all sorts of firms like Gartner,[15] Forrester Research,[16] and 451 Research[17] that review and rank these tools, you'll be far more secure by selecting one than skipping them entirely. Figure 4.2 shows the Gartner Magic Quadrant for endpoint protection platforms. This can be an excellent starting point to identify vendors if you are unfamiliar with the industry.

Expect to pay anywhere from $20 to $150 per endpoint per year for many of these solutions.

Most likely you can go purchase a product after reading this chapter, but how will you respond to alerts? Once you migrate from an EPP to an EDR there are several key points to understand. Many EPPs are mostly "set it and forget it." You install the product and it just works in the background with little to no interaction from you. EDR, however, requires care and feeding. The system must be tuned, and alerts that are generated must be addressed. In this case a managed detection and response (MDR) capability is needed.

▧ MANAGED DETECTION AND RESPONSE

Nearly all of the commercial EDR vendors we previously mentioned offer a managed solution you can add on to your purchase. These vendors have

CHALLENGERS

LEADERS

Microsoft

CrowdStrike

Symantec

Trend Micro

Sophos

ESET

McAfee

Kaspersky

BlackBerry Cylance

Bitdefender

FireEye Cisco

Carbon Black

F-Secure Panda Security

SentinelOne

Palo Alto Networks

Check Point Software Technologies

Fortinet

Malwarebytes

NICHE PLAYERS

VISIONARIES

COMPLETENESS OF VISION →

ABILITY TO EXECUTE

As of August 2019   © Gartner, Inc

Source: Gartner (August 2019)

FIGURE 4.2 Magic Quadrant for Endpoint Protection Platforms

realized that this is something companies that are constrained on people resources want, and these EDR vendors want to sell to start-ups like you with no cybersecurity staff to speak of.

I recommend using these services once you are beyond 45 employees and typically until you have a cybersecurity team in-house. The services offered from each individual vendor does provide a higher degree of services, as they are experts in their own tools. But as you scale, this may get to the point where it is now more complex to manage many vendors that are managing each individual solution you have in place. Not only do

EDR vendors offer this but many more cybersecurity vendors are moving toward this trend.

As your start-up scales, anywhere between your A and C round of funding and between 200 and 1000 employees, you may have some level of cybersecurity team. And the "rule of 3 and 10" for start-ups also applies to cybersecurity in your start-up. The defenses you had in place with 3 employees will break at 10 and then again at 30 and again at 100. At this point it may be beneficial to migrate to a single MDR vendor that is agnostic to your technology stack and that can take over those responsibilities from those individual vendors.

When migrating from a vendor managed solution, where the EDR vendor is managing that specific solution for you, to a vendor that will manage many cybersecurity tools there are several things to consider. As you scale and buy new products, these can become complex and expensive to replace. Not all MDR vendors are agnostic to your technology stack. Some will have partnered with specific vendors, and they will only manage those specific vendors.

As you grow your start-up and mature the cybersecurity capabilities, you will need the right amount of support. The option to hire isn't always an option. This is the real value proposition of an MDR provider. Until you are issuing devices to users or have an MVP product running in a cloud provider you most likely won't need an MDR. But when you do meet or pass those thresholds it is time to consider this purchase.

When looking for an MDR vendor you will find two primary types: those that will support any vendor of your choosing, and those that will prescribe the vendor for the specific solution you are looking for. Typically, an MDR might manage the follow types of systems:

- Endpoint Detection and Response (EDR)
- Security Incident Event Management (SIEM)
- Email Security Gateway (SEG)[18]
- Firewalls
- Vulnerability scanners
- Cloud Security Posture Management (CSPM)

It is important to note what tools they will and will not manage and their response to alerts or events. The name "managed detection and response" can be misleading. You will find some vendors that fall in the MDR vendor category that will respond to alerts in your SIEM but will

Scope of MDR Services

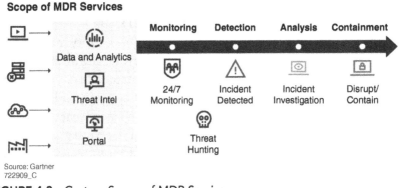

Source: Gartner
722909_C

FIGURE 4.3 Gartner Scope of MDR Services

not manage it. This is a small but critical detail, as there can be a lot of time-consuming work in keeping a tool like that functioning.

You will also want to have a very clear understanding of their playbooks and how they build those for each customer. No two companies are alike and the bespoke nature of MDRs are actualized during the onboarding processes, when they are learning and documenting your environment. A unique limitation of these vendors is the inability to do a proof of concept (POC) or proof of value (POV). Because of the high amount of engineering to build a single customer environment, a typical POV of 30 or 60 days is just not realistic across a broad set of cybersecurity tools.

Your best bet in these situations is to build in strong termination clauses in your favor at specific intervals and treat your first year of service as a paid proof of value.[19] This is usually win-win for both you and the vendor. You have the ability to stop paying if things don't work out and the vendor doesn't lose engineering hours from the bulk of work in building your environment. Figure 4.3 shows the typical scope of responsibilities for the MDR you select.

 ## CASE STUDY

Venrs (pronounced "veneers") is a four-year-old start-up founded by two dental school dorm roommates, Teagan and Hanna. Venrs allows customers to get their own temporary teeth veneers in the comfort of their home through a unique teeth mold kit they've developed. Venrs has raised a total of $115 million in three rounds with an annual reoccurring revenue (ARR) of $24 million.

Venrs stores a large number of customer health records. With 300 employees, it has been overwhelming for their IT and DevOps teams to manage the antivirus on employee laptops and the security in their cloud environment that stores customer electronic private health information (ePHI). Teagan, Hanna, and other executive team members that are part of their board of directors decided at the last end-of-year board meeting to delay hiring an internal cybersecurity team for one more year.

While this choice made their pitch deck numbers very attractive in their five-year forecast to investors in their most recent capital round, it also impacted team performance.

Recently, the DevOps team had to fight off bot attacks on their customer portal from credential stuffing attacks. And IT has been spending hundreds of hours a week troubleshooting issues with the SMB-grade antivirus they've been using since founding the company. Bishop, CTO of Venrs, who is responsible for DevOps and IT, brings these issues to the next executive staff meeting.

Bishop has pulled together several concerning metrics for the meeting. Over the last 16 months, IT spent 67% of their time supporting the antivirus solution they are using. While the cost for licensing was extremely low, they've spent 1200% of FTE costs supporting the tool. The IT team also believes they are missing threats in the environment due to the lack of capabilities of the current solution. However, replacing the old technology with modern EDR will increase license cost and still require maintenance by the IT team. Teagan and Hanna ask for a third option. Bishop also prepared options for outsourcing both the EDR tools, and the monitoring and management, to an MDR provider. With the 300 employee laptops and 15 Kubernetes[20] clusters running in production, the MDR solution would have minimal impact on their five-year forecasting.

SUMMARY

EDR is the new antivirus for our computers. The end goal is the same in that it should protect your device from common and advanced threats that could put your start-up at risk. While Windows comes with Microsoft Defender by default, you still need protection for your MacOS and Linux-based systems.

If you can find a solution that works across your entire environment, that's great. But don't be surprised when you have to sacrifice ease of management for best-in-class solutions. While many of the vendors we mentioned do support Windows, MacOS, and Linux, some focus specifically on one operating system and do it very well.

ACTION PLAN

- Determine what operating systems you need to support.
- Determine if you need the solution managed; this will depend on whether you are in the formation, validation, or growth stage.
- Review terms and conditions with your general counsel.
- Be cautious locking into long-term contracts if you have not used the vendor before. If cost is the reason to purchase a 3-year term then make sure you have strong termination rights.
- Deploy the solution as soon as possible.
- Go back again to Chapter 2 and your roadmap, add any additional needs to the document you created.

NOTES

1. Sandboxing is the technique of logically isolating a file, application, process, etc. from the system it is on, in an attempt to prevent malicious actions.
2. Host-based Intrusion Prevent System came about prior to EDR and was an early predecessor to behavior-based detection capabilities.
3. https://www.crowdstrike.com/
4. https://www.carbonblack.com/
5. https://www.blackberry.com/us/en/products/blackberry-protect
6. https://www.sentinelone.com/
7. https://www.microsoft.com/en-us/windows/comprehensive-security
8. https://www.fireeye.com/products/endpoint-security.html
9. https://www.trendmicro.com/en_us/business.html

10. https://capsule8.com/
11. https://www.limacharlie.io/
12. https://wazuh.com/
13. https://bluespawn.cloud/
14. https://openedr.com/
15. https://www.gartner.com
16. https://go.forrester.com/
17. https://451research.com
18. Not all vendors in the email security space are now considered SEG or call themselves SEG. Many vendors now have the ability to perform the same functions either through APIs or specific marketplace apps available from popular providers like Google Workspace and Microsoft Office 365.
19. Proof of concept and proof of value are used interchangeably to describe the time period in which you will use a solution to determine whether you will purchase it.
20. "Kubernetes, also known as K8s, is an open-source system for automating deployment, scaling, and management of containerized applications." – www.kubernetes.io

CHAPTER FIVE

Your Office Network

Complexity is the worst enemy of security, and our systems are getting more complex all the time.

– Bruce Schneier, *Data and Goliath:*
The Hidden Battles to Collect Your Data
and Control Your World

N THE AGE OF CLOUD and software-as-a-service (SaaS), the need for a defined network perimeter with demilitarized zones (DMZs)[1] and firewalls is blurred or completely gone. Cybersecurity is a layered effort and must address risks at all levels of your business, both operations and technical. As you work your way out from the thing you want to produce you will eventually make your way to the network, where all your data travels and transverses. This can be your home router and Internet connection with you and your fellow founders, or a shared workspace or private office. Each brings similar and unique risks.

When you launch your start-up you might be working from a home office, garage, or friend's couch. In an environment that you own, and where you control the router you connect to such as your Wi-Fi, or plug directly into, it is a bit easier to ensure a higher level of security. The basics, like making sure you change the default login password, update the firmware or operating system, and enable any security features that are offered, are essential to keeping your network secure.

YOUR FIRST OFFICE SPACE

Your first office space, where you sign a lease or buy a building, something that is not your living room, spare bedroom, or garage, is an exciting time in the life of a start-up. While designing the physical space, colors, vending machines, and cold brew coffee on tap is fun, you can't leave out your network. You'll most likely work with a subcontractor that wires everything in your office to include the Internet.

While your new office will most likely have networking wired throughout, you will probably have a wireless network for ease of use. Most modern start-ups with an office space will have people moving through that space all day. Being tied to an ethernet cable just doesn't happen that much today. Especially in a large conference room when you are performing a retro of your most recent feature sprint, you are unlikely to have 12 ethernet jacks to plug into.

The wireless network equipment industry has gone through a bit of consolidation, so there are a handful of enterprise vendors you will have to choose from. There is really no wrong choice, and future planning for a space you just moved into can be difficult for a wireless network. The contractor you work with should be able to help you determine how many people might be in the space at peak times, and then help you select the right equipment. Figure 5.1 shows the Gartner Magic Quadrant for wired and wireless network infrastructure, which is a great place to start when evaluating vendors. Some vendors in this space are:

- Ubiquiti[2]
- Cisco Meraki[3]
- Aruba[4]

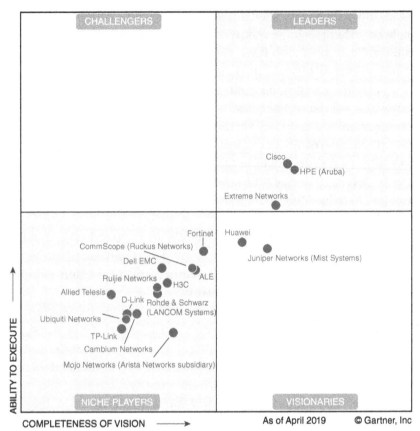

FIGURE 5.1 Magic Quadrant for the Wired and Wireless LAN Access Infrastructure
Source: Gartner

They will also take into consideration voice over IP phones if you will have desk phones, conference room coverage, and things like smart TVs[5] or other streaming devices. If you have three conference rooms and all three are being used to stream a meeting, that's a lot of wireless bandwidth.

Then, obviously, comes security. All the top enterprise vendors have many built-in security features as well as ones you can purchase as a software module as you scale and your needs change. What you must not do is purchase a home or soho device. If you are moving into an official office space you should not be on a wireless system designed for the home. These lack the robust security features an enterprise network requires. Once an attacker has access to your network, they have a massive advantage over all other security controls in place.

If you are going it on your own and bootstrapping your wireless network, it will be in your best interest to get intimately familiar with configuration best practices for that device. If you have high availability and redundancy requirements, look for equipment that can support two or more internet service providers (ISP). If your ISP goes down, you will lose Internet access. If the cost isn't a concern, then subscribing to two different providers to reduce the risk of losing Internet access completely might be of value.

It is also far easier to set up virtual local area networks (VLANs) from the very start. Logically separating teams or departments can help prevent an attacker moving quickly through your network if they gain a foothold on an employee's device on your network.

Enable all of the security controls available to you in the platform you have purchased. If you start with everything turned on, it will save significant time as you scale. Instead of starting with your network wide open and then trying to implement security after you have tens or hundreds of users on the network, people will build with the security controls. If you implement the security controls after the fact you will run the risk of breaking something that utilized the completely open network.

Of the small list of enterprise vendors I mentioned previously, both Ubiquiti and Cisco make consumer and prosumer[6] equipment. While these devices might support robust speeds, these should not be used in the place of enterprise equipment. If you are moving into an office space where you will be responsible for the network equipment, you will want to work with a vendor to help deploy and manage the equipment. At the enterprise level these devices are not "set it and forget it." Start-ups can move into a leased office space almost at any point in the start-up life cycle, so it is difficult to say definitively when you should be large enough to hire a full-time network engineer.

We discussed management of endpoint detection and response (EDR) in Chapter 4, but there are also vendors that help with managing your network. This is important, as now almost every enterprise wireless network vendor provides either built-in security functions or makes software licenses available for upgrading to those features. These controls will generate alerts just like your EDR and will need to be monitored and responded to.

When you prepare for audits and certifications, discussed in detail in Chapter 9, the evidence that you will provide to show you respond to alerts will help you pass your audit. Showing an auditor a system where there are unactioned alerts for many months will make the audit process more time consuming, expensive, and painful.

 ## CO-WORKING SPACES

The advent of shared space, subleases, and other vendors like WeWork introduce a new challenge to start-up network security. You will most likely have no control over these network environments, and it can be very expensive if you want the leasing company to provide your own segmented wireless network. The best course of action if you are working from a space like this is to treat it like a public wireless network at a coffee shop.

Make sure you read Chapters 3 and 4 again if you are in this type of space and you do not control the shared network. It will be important to make sure your devices and accounts are secure before connecting to these networks. You could use things like virtual private networks (VPN), which we discuss next, but these can introduce latency and other management complexities if not deployed properly.

Verify your devices are fully patched, unnecessary services are disabled, and you have either EDR or EPP (discussed in Chapter 4) installed and enabled before connecting to these networks. Depending on your scale once moving into one of these spaces, if budget allows, looking into cloud access security brokers (CASB) and secure access service edge (SASE) can be a very good alternative to legacy VPN to access things like your development and staging environments in your cloud infrastructure provider.

Some example vendors in these spaces are:

- Fyde (Barracuda CloudGen Access)[7]
- Zscaler[8]
- Forcepoint[9]
- NetSkope[10]
- HashiCorp Boundry[11]

VIRTUAL PRIVATE NETWORK

To VPN or not to VPN, that is the question. A virtual private network is a software-based solution you would typically install on your device, laptop, phone, or tablet. There are hardware-based VPNs that large enterprises use to connect two or more remote offices. But you will most likely come across software-based VPNs. A VPN is not the be-all and end-all to cybersecurity or privacy. Turning on a VPN doesn't suddenly make your system more secure or more antifragile.

Let's talk about some basic examples. When you connect to your bank's website it uses transport layer security (TLS), which is the S in HTTPS. This ensures the data you send between your bank and your computer are secure and private. However, in a shared network like the one we discussed previously, an attacker on that network could see that you visit the Acme Bank Co. website, but they would not be able to see what you did on that website.

A more abstract way to talk about it is that Alice and Bob (of cybersecurity fame[12]) are having a conversation in a conference room with glass walls and the door open. You are standing outside the room and can hear the conversation. You see Alice and Bob, and can hear what they are saying. This is like going to Acme Bank Co. using no TLS, completely unencrypted. Someone on the same network could see you visit the site and see what you do there.

Now Alice and Bob shut the door. For simplicity, let's assume the room is completely soundproof. You can still see Alice and Bob talking, but you cannot hear the conversation anymore. This is like visiting Acme Bank Co using TLS and HTTPS. Someone on the same network can see you visit the site but cannot see what you did there.

Now all the blinds are shut to the conference room and there are one or more other entrances. You have no idea if Alice and Bob are in there or what they are talking about. You have no idea who is talking to who. This is like VPN. The VPN creates a private connection to a VPN server; somewhere on the Internet, your traffic flows completely concealed from your system to this VPN. It then leaves the VPN server to the initial website you requested, Acme Bank Co.

But can't the VPN server see where I am going? That depends on the VPN service you use. There are literally hundreds to select from and all meet different needs. If you just want to hide your traffic in your shared working space, most of the popular ones will do. If you are a reporter in a country that targets journalists for political arrest, you will want a very strong VPN that very clearly explains what they do with your data.

There are also vulnerabilities in these VPN providers that must be mentioned but this is a larger topic, and beyond the scope of this book. A common one is what is called leaking domain name server (DNS) requests. This is the request your computer sends to ask for the internet protocol (IP) address of a website like Acme Bank Co. If it is important to conceal all your traffic, you will want to make sure the VPN service tunnels all of your traffic. Figure 5.2 shows the differences and overlaps between several popular remote access technologies.

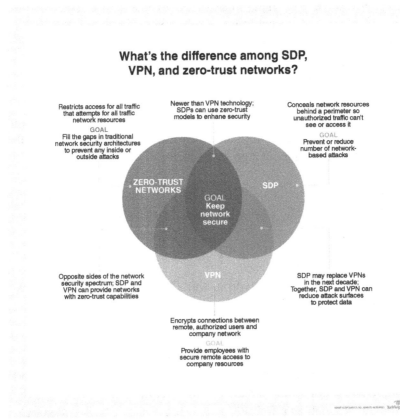

What's the difference among SDP, VPN, and zero-trust networks?

Restricts access for all traffic that attempts for all traffic network resources
GOAL
Fill the gaps in traditional network security architectures to prevent any inside or outside attacks

Newer than VPN technology; SDPs can use zero-trust models to enhane security

Conceals network resources behind a perimeter so unauthorized traffic can't see or access it
GOAL
Prevent or reduce number of network-based attacks

ZERO-TRUST NETWORKS

SDP

GOAL
Keep network secure

Opposite sides of the network security spectrum; SDP and VPN can provide networks with zero-trust capabilities

VPN

SDP may replace VPNs in the next decade; Together, SDP and VPN can reduce attack surfaces to protect data

Encrypts connections between remote, authorized users and company network
GOAL
Provide employees with secure remote access to company resources

FIGURE 5.2 Comparison of SDP, VPN, and Zero-Trust Networks
Source: https://searchnetworking.techtarget.com/feature/SDP-vs-VPN-vs-zero-trust-networks-Whats-the-difference

SUMMARY

You'll have a network of some kind in every phase of the life of your start-up. From your wireless network at home; shared wireless network in a co-working space; or eventually your own office, floor, or entire building. Each of these brings different threats and security controls that should be implemented.

All of these network devices will have some type of login; use your knowledge from Chapter 3, "Secure Your Credentials," to make sure these devices are secure from the start. Turning on all the offered security features when possible is a great idea. Waiting until there are 200 people on the network in your new office is the wrong time to start turning on these features, which could negatively impact users. And when that happens these settings tend to just remain turned off.

 ACTION PLAN

- Make sure your home wireless router has strong authentication setup, a passphrase you store in your password manager. If it is controlled through a cloud app, turn on multi-factor authentication if that is an option.
- Before you move into a co-working space or use a public wireless network make sure your device is secure, as we discussed in Chapters 3 and 4.
- Turn on all security features on your enterprise wireless network when you move into a leased space.
- Consider adding any items from this Chapter to your roadmap you started building in Chapter 2.

 NOTES

1. Demilitarized zones were popular up to the early 2000s as a networking configuration to segment systems that needed to be accessible to the public, such as a website, away from sensitive back end systems, such as your customer database.
2. https://www.ui.com/

3. https://meraki.cisco.com/
4. https://www.arubanetworks.com/
5. Check the privacy settings on any smart TVs in your office. In some cases, they have been able to record audio and video without the user's knowledge. You don't want that happening in your board meetings.
6. Prosumer is a term used to describe technology that sits between consumer technology and enterprise technology. It typically has more features and capabilities than a consumer device you might find in a person's home and less or more affordable comparable features to high-end enterprise solutions.
7. https://www.fyde.com/
8. https://www.zscaler.com/
9. https://www.forcepoint.com/
10. https://www.netskope.com/
11. https://www.boundaryproject.io/
12. The names Alice and Bob have been used in various technology examples and books for years.

CHAPTER SIX

Your Product in the Cloud

There is no cloud, it's just someone else's computer.

– Anonymous

U NDOUBTEDLY, IF YOU ARE READING this book you are most likely building a company that will be hosted in the cloud. The cloud, simply put, is a service that provides the underlying infrastructure to host whatever system or application you might be building. Also referred to as infrastructure-as-a-service (IaaS), this service usually includes the management of servers and data centers. There are many large providers in this space, including Amazon Web Services (AWS),[1] Microsoft Azure,[2] Google Cloud Platform (GCP),[3] IBM Cloud,[4] Oracle Cloud,[5] and Alibaba Cloud.[6] This takes all the pain of managing a data center, and even the servers in the data center, away from the customer and allows you to build and host your product in a fast and convenient way. Figure 6.1 shows the Gartner Magic Quadrant for cloud infrastructure as a service.

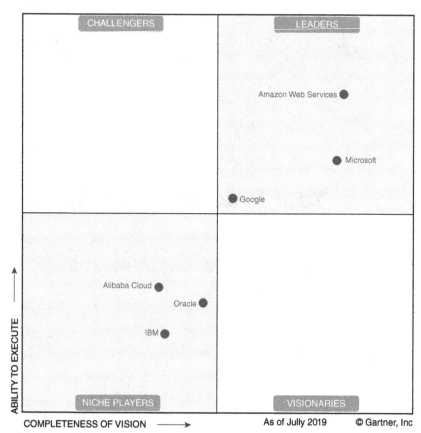

FIGURE 6.1 Magic Quadrant for Cloud Infrastructure as a Service
Source: Gartner

All of these provide nearly the same services with a few key differences in unique capabilities. Regardless of the provider you select you should closely follow their recommended security configurations for both your account and systems within your account. Like many of the topics in this book, implementing these controls at the beginning will pay dividends in the future.

Properly configured cloud environments, from the very start, can delay or completely offset future costs of both people and technology to help with managing the security controls in your cloud environment.

I'm not saying you should avoid hiring a cloud security architect or deploying a cloud security management platform (CSMP); you will eventually need them.

 ## SECURE YOUR CLOUD PROVIDER ACCOUNTS

There are many components to cloud environments and one of those is the actual account you use to manage this solution. We discussed in Chapter 3 how critical strong passphrases and multi-factor authentication (MFA) are. This is absolutely an account you must protect with the maximum available security controls. All of the providers we've mentioned in this book offer the ability to protect your account. The label of this account might differ; for example, in AWS this is called the root account. This account has total control over the environment. Under no circumstances should this account be used to build and manage the environment on a daily basis. All of these providers offer some type of granular access control and you should create individual accounts with only the access and entitlements that they need, nothing more. This applies to service accounts that would be used programmatically, and never used by an individual engineer.

Some may even have the ability to have multiple owners or administrators for your specific account. Just like we discussed in Chapter 3 about entitlements, there are many different ones in each of the major cloud provider platforms. While we can't detail each one here, in the footnote are the links to the major providers we've mentioned and their recommended best practices for protecting your user account.[7]

Once you've created secure accounts to access your cloud environment you will want to follow the recommended best practices when building that infrastructure. Each provider is a bit different but some of the basics include:

- Using the latest workload images available that are fully patched.
- Enabling auto-patching if possible.
- Setting granular network security rules. This would normally be firewall rules in a traditional datacenter; your provider may call it a different name. You want to avoid allowing all traffic. Starting out with deny-all and adding only specific allow rules is best.

The settings in all of these providers are expansive, granular, and numerous in number. There are, of course, vendors that help you manage this as well, called cloud security posture management (CSPM). These tools can help to not only monitor your cloud account configuration but also take corrective action. For example, in AWS the popular storage function called simple storage service (S3) can be set to public and unencrypted. This can have a valid business reason for being configured in such a way, but most of the time you want your S3 buckets to be private and encrypted.

In the world of DevOps and enabling developers to move fast you don't always have a mechanism to prevent things from being configured a certain way. With CSPM you can be alerted to such events and even take an automated corrective action, such as automatically detecting, then setting, an S3 bucket to private and encrypting it as in our previous example.

▨ PROTECT YOUR WORKLOADS

Most cloud providers (infrastructure-as-a-service, IaaS) refer to a running system as a workload or simply compute. Think of this as a traditional Linux or Windows server running in their virtualized environment. Regardless of the provider you go with, you will most likely be running Linux or Windows. Starting from scratch has a lot of benefits. This is one of the most difficult areas in which to go back and add security later. And as the years go by, it gets exponentially more difficult, expensive, and risky.

There is also low risk of getting locked into one or another cybersecurity vendor to protect your workloads, as any limitations can be addressed through engineering. When you build the system securely from the start it guides your engineering teams to build a product within those requirements from the start.

This is also an area where you will want to consider the MDR solutions we discussed in Chapter 4. In the formation stage you may not have a cybersecurity team but it is very possible you have an MVP with active customers using it. This will be too much of a burden to manage in-house, and finding either an EDR vendor with an MDR offering or an agnostic MDR to assist will be critical to scaling security on your workloads. Figure 6.2 shows the

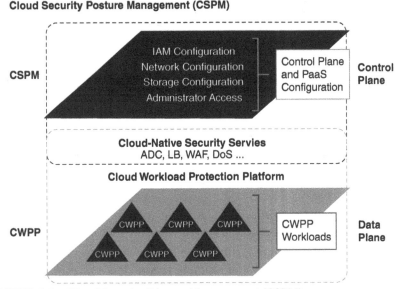

FIGURE 6.2 Cloud Security Posture Management (CSPM)
Source: Gartner

differences of cloud security posture management and cloud workload protection platforms.

Patching

The single greatest thing you can do, starting from scratch like this, is to get automated patching in place. Building into your build pipeline the requirement of always deploying patched and updated software will pay dividends long into the future. Obviously, you still need to follow standard continuous development/continuous integration (CD/CI) processes when moving code from dev, test, quality assurance (QA), staging, and finally to production. Your automatic patching, when applied through that same life cycle, will allow you to move much more quickly when patches are released, and they will always be released.

There are numerous books on DevOps, so we won't go too deep into that subject here. However, there are many different solutions to automate

	Source	Cloud	Type	Infrastructure	Language	Agent	Master	Community	Maturity
Chef	Open	All	Config Mgmt	Mutable	Procedural	Yes	Yes	Large	High
Puppet	Open	All	Config Mgmt	Mutable	Declarative	Yes	Yes	Large	High
Ansible	Open	All	Config Mgmt	Mutable	Procedural	No	No	Huge	Medium
SaltStack	Open	All	Config Mgmt	Mutable	Declarative	Yes	Yes	Large	Medium
CloudFormation	Closed	AWS	Provisioning	Immutable	Declarative	No	No	Small	Medium
Heat	Open	All	Provisioning	Immutable	Declarative	No	No	Small	Low
Terraform	Open	All	Provisioning	Immutable	Declarative	No	No	Huge	Low

FIGURE 6.3   Comparison of Popular Fleet Management Solutions
Source: https://blog.gruntwork.io/why-we-use-terraform-and-not-chef-puppet-
ansible-saltstack-or-cloudformation-7989dad2865c?gi=ecd4f8e433e4

patching in your environment. If you are rolling your own operating system image and not using a fleet management tool, like Puppet, Chef, or Ansible, then creating an automated cycle will be necessary to make sure a patch does not break something in production. Figure 6.3 shows a high-level comparison of just some of the fleet management tools available to start-ups today.

Endpoint Protection

We discussed endpoint protection for your laptop and mobile devices in Chapter 4. These products typically support your cloud workloads as well. There are also very specific point products in that their only function is to protect these systems. This is something you will want to prioritize once you are in the validation phase and should absolutely have in place in growth and beyond. The start-up phases are good indicators here, and in addition to those, regardless of phase, if you are running your product in production with customers using it, you should have an endpoint detection and response (EDR) plan in place already.

This is highly subjective, depending on what operating system your workload is running on. When speaking with vendors, you will want to dig in here to understand what is truly supported by their product. You may find the kernel (the kernel is the heart and brain of your operating system and controls all functions of it) version you are on, or even the distribution of Linux (there are many) you are using, are not supported. Since this will be running in your production environment you should understand how it could impact your system. Some products require that they are installed as a kernel module (this is a piece of code or software that adds additional functionality to the operating system kernel) and some may only need system-level access in order to access the specific system calls they need to detect and block threats.

SECURE YOUR CONTAINERS

Kubernetes, Docker, Mesos, CoreOS, and many others make it very easy to build robust applications very quickly and make things very portable. Containers allow you to build and ship code very quickly and also make it extremely portable. The container should contain just the libraries and packages your application needs to run. Containers allow you to run your code from anywhere that can run the container, all without having to worry about how the underlying operating system is configured. And like the workloads or compute these containers run on, the container must also be secured. There are even more vendors in this space; some overlap with others we discussed and some are only focused on containers. And not all of them support all types of containers. Figure 6.4 shows a high-level example of how container orchestration works.

Without going through what products support which containers, the first step is making sure you are following the recommended best practices from that container to secure it from the start. Containers are also not immune to patching. You will need to apply the same principles as you did to workloads and compute. Including a vulnerable library in your container still makes it vulnerable.

There are both free open source solutions and commercial solutions that can be integrated into your build pipeline that will scan your container at build time and before it is pushed to production. These scans can check for common misconfigurations as well as vulnerabilities within the container. You should make it a requirement and habit that no container is pushed to production if it contains vulnerabilities. Trying to implement this requirement years later will most likely result in software engineers being pulled off product-related work to go back and retool systems to support this critical capability.

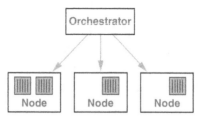

FIGURE 6.4 Depiction of Container Orchestration
Source: https://devopedia.org/container-orchestration

 SUMMARY

If you are building a product that will be hosted in the cloud, all the same cybersecurity principles still apply. The technology changes a bit but you still need to focus on protecting the data, the systems the data lives on, and the people that have access to the systems and data.

Turning on available security controls in your cloud provider account as soon as possible will make engineering your product within a secure environment far easier than trying to do it after the growth phase. And both your workloads, the servers that applications run on and the containers that run on those workloads, must also be built in a way that allows for never-ending vendor patches to be applied without disrupting productions.

Properly configured cloud environments can be built by hand following the vendor's documentation, but there is always room for error if you've never worked in that environment. This is a good place to possibly engage outside help in verifying the design and architecture.

 ACTION PLAN

- Apply what you learned in Chapter 3 to your cloud account. Protect those credentials at all costs and use them only for their recommended purpose as directed by your cloud provider.
- Enable multi-factor authentication on your cloud provider account.
- If possible, use the most up-to-date workload images supplied by the cloud provider. If your product needs something more bespoke, make

sure you've accounted for how you will patch it when it is running in production.

- If you have already selected an endpoint detection and response solution, which we dove into in Chapter 4, and it supports your cloud workloads, deploy it as you are building the product. You want to make sure it does not interfere with what you are building. Pay attention to resource usage by the EDR and central processing unit (CPU); memory and disk space all cost money.
- If you are building a fully containerized environment, make sure you are again accounting for patching. Vendors are not perfect and will always release patches. Your product should account for this.
- Take any findings from this Chapter and go back to Chapter 2 and the roadmap you started on and add those items to the roadmap.

NOTES

1. https://aws.amazon.com/
2. https://azure.microsoft.com/
3. https://azure.microsoft.com/
4. https://www.ibm.com/cloud
5. https://www.oracle.com/cloud/
6. https://www.alibabacloud.com/
7. https://aws.amazon.com/blogs/security/getting-started-follow-security-best-practices-as-you-configure-your-aws-resources/; https://docs.microsoft.com/en-us/azure/security/fundamentals/best-practices-and-patterns; https://cloud.google.com/security/best-practices; https://www.ibm.com/cloud/security; https://www.alibabacloud.com/help/faq-detail/56346.htm.

7

Information Technology

Don't assume a crack is too small to be noticed, or too small to be exploited.

– Rob Joyce, Tailored Access Operations, NSA

NFORMATION TECHNOLOGY, OR IT, can mean different things to different people. We'll refer to IT in this book in the sense of the technology and people that are part of our corporate environments. We are specifically excluding cloud environments like Amazon Web Services (AWS), Microsoft Azure, or Google Cloud Platform (GCP) when talking about IT.

Things we might associate with IT in a typical corporate environment might be people like helpdesk staff, network engineers and administrators, desktop engineers and administrators, and the like. Some technology associated with this team are our laptops, printers, network switches, and Internet access, among other things.

As a scaling start-up, you probably won't have these people or teams, but most likely will have a laptop and Internet access. So, you and your co-founders will be the ones doing tech support, along with securing your start-up while you build your product. IT, however, is not what it used to be 30 years ago, or even 10 years ago. Reporting structures have shifted from chief financial officers (CFO), because IT was once the largest cost center, to the chief information officer (CIO). IT was also responsible for data centers, but with the advent of cloud infrastructure-as-a-service (IaaS) and DevOps, the responsibilities have bifurcated. DevOps and the site reliability engineers (SRE) on that team are the ones responsible for that new breed of data center technology.

The roles and responsibilities of IT are again shifting. Many organizations put cybersecurity or information security subordinate to IT. As businesses have experienced exponential risk growth directly correlated to cyber risk the roles are now reversing. As more companies move to cloud-based-everything and nearly every start-up builds its company with cloud-based services, IT risks have greatly diminished. Knowing what laptop is assigned to what employee is more critical today for managing cybersecurity risk than it is IT risk. This is also true for managing identities within your start-up. Knowing who has been provisioned in a system and, even more importantly, knowing who has been deprovisioned from a system is purely a cybersecurity risk today. We will most likely see this trend grow more quickly in start-ups where it is mostly greenfield (completely new) and there are no political land grabs necessary to properly address risk for the business.

ASSET MANAGEMENT

Knowing what systems and resources are part of your environment is critical to cybersecurity. Once you are past the growth phase, with maybe several hundred employees, this becomes difficult at best. Asset management not only supports cybersecurity so you can verify 100% coverage of your cybersecurity controls, but also is a requirement in any cybersecurity certifications and standards. We discuss these more in Chapter 9 and Chapter 10.

Asset management is simply the catalog of what devices, laptops, tablets, phones, printers, or monitors that a company owns. And most importantly, who those devices are assigned to in your start-up. This is really easy to track when it is you and two other founders. This is not easy to track in a spreadsheet with 500 employees. When you get to the point of going through an audit you will have a very bad time if you are tracking things via a spreadsheet. The probability of human error increases as you add more and more manual steps. Missing one out of 500 users when deprovisioning someone from your email system is an immediate nonconformity or exception on an audit.

Many solutions exist specifically for asset management and some have additional functionality to track logical access in your start-up as well. This is sometimes referred to as mobile device management (MDM), enterprise mobility management (EMM), or unified endpoint management (UEM). While many of these vendors cover more than mobile smartphones and tablets, the initial solutions were designed for those devices in mind. Figure 7.1 shows the differences and overlapping capabilities of UEM, EMM, and MDM.

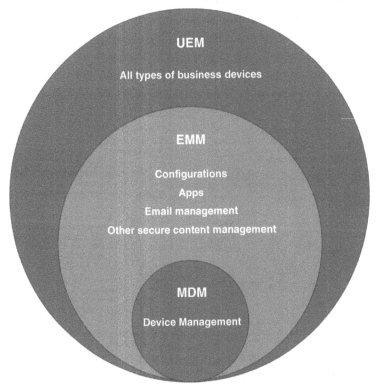

FIGURE 7.1 Depiction of the Differences between MDM, EMM, and UEM
Source: https://blog.codeproof.com/difference-between-mdm-emm-and-uem/

▦ IDENTITY AND ACCESS MANAGEMENT

We talked about our credentials, our keys to our digital selves, in Chapter 3, and a bit about how that scales. Managing users in your start-up requires accurate accounting of onboarding, job role changes, and, most importantly, offboarding. This is commonly referred to as joiners, movers, and leavers (JML). When you hire new people they will have various accounts and access; this provisioning will most likely be manual from formation to validation in the start-up life cycle. Once you are in the growth phase and beyond, you will most likely need to automate this.

Automation is even more critical when deprovisioning users. When someone leaves the company, regardless of the reason, you must have complete confidence that all of their access has been removed. Every audit I have been through in my career has had a finding around users not being properly removed from the environment. This is systemic because automation was not prioritized from the start. Figure 7.2 depicts how identity management may work in a typical organization.

Your identity typically will start with the email provider you select, such as Google or Microsoft. These are some of the most popular solutions

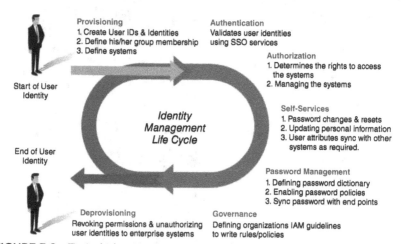

FIGURE 7.2 Typical Identity Management Life Cycle
Source: https://www.innominds.com/blog/open-source-tools-for-identity-and-access-management

that provide numerous integrations into other tools and solutions. These providers don't always provide out-of-the-box support to link your credentials for email to your credentials on your laptop. In Chapter 3 we saw the necessity to reduce the number of passphrases we need to remember and this is one of those occurrences.

You and your founders may have started the company on Apple MacBooks but, as you scale, your environment will become more diverse. For example, your finance team will most likely require Windows-based laptops, as the tools that team uses typically only run on that operating system. This is critical to consider when deciding on a solution to create a seamless experience as you grow from 10 employees to 500 and beyond.

There are also single sign-on (SSO) providers that extend the features and capabilities that might be provided by your identity providers like Google and Microsoft. You most likely won't need to consider a dedicated SSO provider until 500 employees and beyond, or if you are building a B2B application where your customers will most likely expect the solution to support single sign-on.

SUMMARY

Information technology is something we are all familiar with; you might even be using an IT asset to read this book right now. Planning for the day when you and your founders are not the IT administrator, helpdesk, and cybersecurity engineer will allow for smooth transitions between phases in your start-up. Planning, both in the sense of putting the right technology in at the right time and also knowing when it is time to either hire an expert or outsource your needs, is a topic that we will talk about in Chapter 8.

Keeping track of assets as well as your employees' identities and access within those assets is important for both compliance and cyber-security. Many successful data breaches today have some component of reusing valid user or system credentials. Staying aware of the increased complexity of managing, monitoring, and maintaining sound practices and procedures will allow you and your founders to build a strong foundation.

ACTION PLAN

- Document as much as you can; the software-as-a-service (SaaS) tools you are already using, like Google Workspace or Microsoft Office 365, can help you stay organized to a point. A good rule of thumb is that once the data no longer fits on one screen in your spreadsheet, it might be time to buy a solution to automatically manage that data.

- Make sure you can always provide a list of all the systems you have – laptops, mobile devices, cloud workloads, containers, and even software libraries you might build into your product. Auditors will want this, and if you are in the small percentage of start-ups that must obtain a certification like SOC2 or ISO 27001 in the formation or validation phase, you will need this information immediately. We talk about these certifications in Chapter 10.

- Take action items from this Chapter and return to Chapter 2 where you started your roadmap document and add those to the document.

PART TWO

Growing the Team

CHAPTER EIGHT

Hiring, Outsourcing, or Hybrid

Your company culture is who you hire, fire, and
promote.

– Dr. Cameron Sepah

HIRING WELL IS THE SINGLE most important thing any company can do. A bad hire in a key position can be devastating and have a long-lasting negative impact to the business in almost every aspect. Dr. Cameron Sepah said it very well: "Your company culture is who you hire, fire, and promote." And I would add to that: company culture is not free snacks, arcade games, or company trips to exotic locations for team building. Who we surround ourselves with to represent us and our business defines the culture. Once you've figured that out you'll need to decide if it makes sense to hire someone full-time, outsource the role in some way, and decide whether to run the search internally, if you have talent acquisition, or use an outside firm.

As a start-up, you must focus on the details. What is your value proposition? Ensure every new role supports that until revenue is positive.

Creating cybersecurity roles will be essential to protecting the business's current and future revenue and brand. However, creating titles for the sake of checking a box will do far more harm in the long run than thoughtful hiring. Many companies today are expected to have a chief information security officer (CISO) that reports directly to the CEO and has total visibility across the enterprise's cybersecurity posture and risk.

But simply bestowing this title on someone with no tactical security experience will be a detriment to your short- and long-term cybersecurity strategy. A brand-new hospital would not place someone in the role of chief of surgery that has never performed a single surgery in their career. So why would you install someone as the CISO that has never performed a penetration test, participated in incident response, or developed secure code?

As you scale, your needs will always change. This is where attention must be paid, because the person you need at 10 employees is different than the person you need at 1000 employees.

CATALYSTS TO HIRING

Internal and external drivers may exist for your specific organization that will dictate whether you should have a CISO full time or could benefit from contracting one out through a CISO-as-a-service provider or seeking experts to provide an advisory role compensated with equity instead of costly and limited capital. Internal drivers such as board members or even experienced employees may say you need one. External forces, such as your customers, may expect you to also have someone in complete control of your cybersecurity. You must trust the person in this role as much as you trust your co-founders.

Other external forces, such as government regulations, may even dictate it; for example, the New York Department of Financial Services Cybersecurity Regulation (23 NYCRR 500). This law, enacted in the state of New York in 2017, requires, among other things, that financial services appoint a chief information security officer. This was the first of its kind but most likely not the last. You can expect other states or even countries to look to copy this law for the financial sector and possibly others. This will certainly disrupt how you do hiring in the formation, validation, and growth stages of your start-up.

GET THE FIRST HIRE RIGHT

Your first security hire will vary from one stage of your company to the next. If, for example, you are in a highly regulated industry, your first security hire might best be someone with hands-on experience in that industry. If you have little to no regulations surrounding how your business runs beyond common law, then a highly technical individual contributor may be the best first hire. Understanding and navigating the highly competitive cybersecurity job market may be something you will want to engage an outside recruiter for and not attempt it on your own, especially if you have no human resource department or talent acquisition. Hiring should be absolutely your number one priority when you choose to add to your start-up team.

In many cases, if you have under 45 employees, or are in the formation or validation phase, an experienced individual contributor may be your best first hire. You will have a lot of technical tactical work to do as you scale, as you have seen from the previous seven chapters. Some key requirements to look for in a candidate at this phase are:

- Ten or more years of experience in cybersecurity
- Hands-on experience with your start-up needs in the next 18– 24 months
- Previous start-up experience

You will almost want someone that will be a little bored at times in their job. Someone who has "been there, done that" will be able to come in and quickly analyze and understand what must be done, versus what should be done. Despite all the work with your recruiter to identify what your start-up needs in a candidate, you typically capture only about 80% of those needs. Once you have an expert in this field on your team, they will identify other gaps you did not think of, or even realized existed – which is why you are hiring them. Dean Williams tells a great story about Lee Iacocca, in his book *Leadership for a Fractured World*. When Lee joined Chrysler, the company was in shambles; he rebuilt it by hiring experts in every position around him and had them tell him what to do. Remember, you are hiring a cybersecurity expert to tell you what to do.

You can expect to pay someone in this role well over $150,000 base annual salary, and somewhere around $300,000 or more total compensation. Titles you might consider will start with principal, fellow, or distinguished security engineer. These are not hard-and-fast rules and compensation will vary depending on location as well as title. But these are both excellent starting points for your search.

Once you have more than 45 employees, or are into the growth phase, it may be time to consider hiring a cybersecurity executive to fill the chief information security officer (CISO) role for your start-up.

Location is another critical consideration. Most software-as-a-service (SaaS) start-ups born in the cloud can function and scale successfully with employees all over the globe. While you might be like these start-ups and are building a remote first start-up, you should at least consider time zones. You will need a high degree of communication with the critical first cybersecurity hire. This will be difficult if you are in New York City and your first cybersecurity hire is in Melbourne, Australia. If you are hiring in the US, your geographic locations will most likely be centered in the areas depicted in the heat map in Figure 8.1.

EXECUTIVE VERSUS INDIVIDUAL CONTRIBUTOR

Let's look at when to hire an individual contributor versus an executive. Very early stage start-ups can benefit from both and you may find yourself hiring both, but as every company is different, so are your needs. In an engineering-focused company that is building a product, having someone that can dive in and execute on work is important to start with a secure product from inception. This hire could keep things going up to around 45 employees. Also remember that, on average, large organizations (1000+ employees) have a ratio of 1:150 of security engineers to employees. As sales begin to ramp up and depending on what industries you sell into, business-to-consumer (B2C), business-to-business (B2B), etc., you will most likely find that the skills of individual contributors don't apply to business logistics. This can be an inflection point when it is time to bring in a level of management for cybersecurity.

Whether it is "head of cybersecurity" or "chief information security officer," a strategic thinker who is part of the executive team will allow

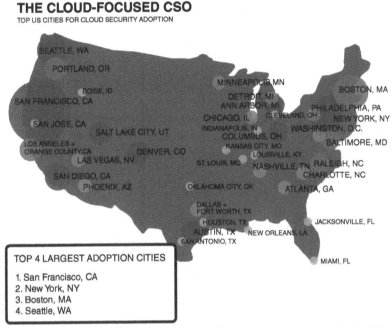

THE CLOUD-FOCUSED CSO
TOP US CITIES FOR CLOUD SECURITY ADOPTION

TOP 4 LARGEST ADOPTION CITIES

1. San Francisco, CA
2. New York, NY
3. Boston, MA
4. Seattle, WA

FIGURE 8.1 Heat Map of Chief Security Officer Hiring Across the United States
Source: https://www.hitchpartners.com/blog

your business to continue to scale securely. Just as individual contributors run the gamut from right out of school to distinguished engineers with 20+ years of experience, so do CISOs. While your company may be very good at hiring individual contributors, a new member of the executive team is not a decision to take lightly or speed through. It is highly recommended to find a firm such as Hitch Partners.[1]

Your recruiter will guide you through this process, and some specifics you should be looking for in candidates are that they have done some or most of what needs to be done. Someone that has experienced building a cybersecurity organization and strategy, especially at a start-up, will be able to understand your unique needs. Certainly, someone with 15 or more years of experience in cybersecurity with a large portion of that in leadership or executive roles. Titles that are either chief information security officer or head of cybersecurity are very common. However, if your first security hire is titled differently, this can signal to candidates that you are not actually ready to hire a cybersecurity executive and that the role is not a priority. Reporting structure is also important, as discussed earlier, because cybersecurity is now a business risk. Who the role reports into can signal either that this position is business critical, or that you are just checking boxes and have no plan to give the role any business authority. These roles should always report in the CEO with some type of accountability to your board. You can expect to pay a CISO anywhere from $600,000 to $1,000,000 total compensation for a mid to late stage start-up.

 ## RECRUITING

Working with a recruiter, whether internal or external, is just that, work. Hiring is not something you just hand off to another individual to do it for you. This should be a collaborative process with you and that individual to help find the best fit for your start-up. This means working together to determine the business needs, translating those needs into a job description, conducting source searches, and interviewing. The steps are mostly the same if you have a talent acquisition team or if you have a retained firm to help in the search.

You'll want to meet with your recruiter to discuss your needs. What types of skills does this person need? Will they be an individual contributor, hands-on middle manager, or executive? Where should the person physically be located? Your recruiter should help you work through this discussion as well if you've never been part of the hiring process before. Once you've developed the requirements and have a full understanding between you and the recruiter of who you need, you'll need to build the job description. A job description is important regardless of hiring an individual contributor or executive.

Lean on your VCs, board members, or advisors to leverage their networks to find the best well-vetted talent to join your team.

 ## JOB DESCRIPTIONS

Writing the job description should be a collaborative process. From the output of your requirements discussion with the recruiter you will either build a draft or they may create a draft for you to then work through the parts and pieces. It's important to remember, the job description might be the first thing your unicorn candidate reads and that is how they are introduced to your unicorn start-up. It's important to be honest and transparent in what you put out as the first touchpoint for possible candidates. It should be inclusive and truthful so individuals can both self-select in or out. Someone reading the job description should be able to tell quickly if this is a job they would want or not. Of course, you'll get the folks that are applying for everything, but you want to make sure those that do apply understand quickly what they are applying for.

Your job description basically needs to be a sales slick sheet. You are in selling mode. You are the one that needs to hire someone. The cybersecurity job market is extremely competitive and will continue to experience that talent shortage well into 2030. It is important to keep this in mind when both writing the job descriptions and interviewing; you need them more than they need you. This is simply the fact of the matter we face as cybersecurity hiring managers.

The job description should be no more than a couple pages at the very most. As hiring managers we always tell people to keep their resume to two or three pages, and this goes for you as a hiring manager and your job description. Starting with a description of the type of person that fits into this role is a great way to clearly and cleanly explain the hard and soft skills needed. Following up with what they will actually do day to day will attract higher quality candidates because they can see exactly what type of work they might be doing each day. I cannot stress enough the importance of being honest and transparent. For example, if you are hiring an individual contributor and they will need to review security logs every day, you should clearly say that. There are many people that like this type of work; there are also many that don't.

Keep the bulleted list of skills, requirements, education, and certifications to a minimum. Don't list every single type of vendor for a specific solution. If you want to say something like Amazon Web Services (AWS) experience is required, that is fine. If you want to make it more general such as "cloud infrastructure-as-a-service (IaaS)," that will cover that type of vendor. But whatever you do, don't just list out every IaaS as a requirement. Even the largest organizations aren't multi-cloud and your start-up most likely is not either.

Education is a tricky topic. Lately there has been a push in the technology sector to remove this requirement to open up the number of possible candidates to a larger, more diverse pool of individuals. You'll have to use your best judgment and work with your recruiter to understand if this is something that should even appear on your job description. If you are asking for a principal security architect with 15 or more years of experience, would a bachelor's in computer science from 15 years ago really be that necessary? The same question can be asked if you are hiring a CISO – do they really require an MBA if you need them to interface with customers, redline customer contracts, and build your cybersecurity program? Give it some thought, but the answer is most likely no.

 INTERVIEWING

I'll keep repeating myself in this chapter to drive home this point: when you decide to hire, this needs to be your number one priority. Whether it is the recruiter or you personally that does the first initial phone screen, this is possibly the first experience this person will have with your company. And if you've read any books about building a successful start-up you will know that customer experience is critical to your brand. That experience starts with how you interact with candidates. You are interviewing them, but they are also interviewing you. As a founder, if this gives you even a moment of pause, you should have someone other than yourself conduct the first initial interview. You need to be in sales mode, and if you know you are not the right salesperson to sell this unicorn hire on joining your start-up, have the right person do it.

Have a process, even if it is just on the back of a napkin. Even if it is as simple as a phone screen with the recruiter, a phone screen with the hiring manager, and then an all-day onsite to meet the rest of the team. Having something documented, even if informally, makes it easier to repeat. Keeping the same process for each candidate helps to truly equally evaluate each person that wants to join your start-up.

Be respectful of the candidate's time. Remember you are selling them on your start-up just as much as they are selling you on themselves. The tech industry trend of marathon interview days, sometimes lasting six or more hours, is simply out of hand. This is in large part due to the trend of one-on-one interviews, where the candidate interviews with multiple people, one at a time over one or more days. This interview strategy can lead to bias in interviews and frustration and annoyance on the candidate's side. Panel interviews capped at two hours in length are far better at fully evaluating a candidate. Rarely will someone ever work one-on-one with individuals in a start-up. It is nearly all teamwork, and so should your interview process be. If you do interview debriefs, you only have an individual's perception to base your judgment on. However, if you were in that interview with your co-founders, you might perceive the answers to questions differently than them.

Be on time. This is the easiest thing you can do for the interview. I've heard too many times from friends and colleagues about an interviewer showing up late to an interview. This is just as important for you as the hiring manager as it is for the candidate. A less experienced individual might just brush it off since they may feel they have less power in this relationship, but somebody with 20 years of experience, an individual contributor or executive, will see this as a red flag. Don't lose out on a great candidate because you couldn't manage your own time properly.

Always ask the same questions in each round of the interview. This is the best way to have an unbiased result at the end of the process and find the best candidate for your start-up. Keeping a structured format is difficult but highly rewarding, as you will increase the possibility of hiring better and more diverse candidates. Unconscious bias is a natural human trait; we all have it, we all do it, and we can all acknowledge it. Having a defined process for interviews ensures we address that head on and guarantees the long-term success of our business. You want someone that is going to see problems different than you and bring different solutions than you would. A great leader is able to source a diverse set of ideas to push their business to the next level.

After each stage of your interview process you should continue to collaborate and meet with your recruiter. They may probe you with questions but you should also share why someone was a great fit or not. This will help your recruiter continue to source candidates that are exactly what your business needs today and into the future.

FIRST 90 DAYS IS A MYTH

It takes well over 90 days for an individual, regardless of experience level, to get fully up to speed in a new job. To completely understand your start-up in and out as well as build political capital will take longer than 90 days. Your only expectation for the first 90 days should be that they get a quick lay of the land and develop a plan based on what they learned in that first 90 days. In a start-up, you are building and moving fast. Enabling this new teammate to do that will be critical to their success as well as yours. If your job description was accurate and your interview process was transparent, they should know exactly what needs to be done when they walk in the door.

 SUMMARY

When you decide to hire your first role for cybersecurity it must be your number one priority. Not only are your first strategic hires important when you are in the formation phase of your start-up, they are even more critical in the validation and growth phase, when the impact of this individual is even greater. There is less room for error with a bad hire, and making sure you and your recruiter are on the same page is an important first step. Defining a hiring plan that includes how interviews will be conducted and ensuring a diverse candidate pool will ensure your start-up moves smoothly from formation all the way to the growth phase.

Hiring is a collaborative process and shouldn't be done in a bubble. Ask for help from your recruiter, peers, network, VC, and co-founders. This decision impacts all of these stakeholders.

 ACTION PLAN

- Define your needs for the candidate.
- Determine if those needs are for an engineer or executive.
- Engage with your talent acquisition partner or recruiting firm.

- If you don't yet have a recruiting firm, begin interviewing recruiting firms that specialize in the type of candidate you are looking for. Not all firms recruit engineers or executives.
- Go back to Chapter 2 again and add hiring plans to your roadmap.

NOTE

1. https://www.hitchpartners.com

PART THREE

Maturation

CHAPTER NINE

Compliance

You have 20 seconds to comply.

– ED-209, Robocop

W HEN A COMPANY IS REQUIRED or chooses to be compliant with a specific standard or framework it is important to understand what compliance means. After completing your first audit, regardless of the standard, and receiving some type of certification or official document you can have an overwhelming feeling of relief and that you are finished. This is not the case. Becoming compliant with a standard can lure you into a false sense of security. Compliance is meant to hold a minimum standard for a sustained period of time. Doing so does not necessarily mean your company is secure.

Nearly all cybersecurity compliance standards and regulations have some form of exception acceptance. It can be time-consuming and costly to achieve a flawless audit and may not benefit you or your customers by having zero exceptions. And just as there are exceptions for audits, there are exceptions to the fact that you may need to have a flawless audit depending on your industry. Highly regulated industries like healthcare, finance, and government contractors in some cases have no choice.

It seems today you can't swing an Ethernet cable without hitting a company that must comply with some type of government regulation or industry compliance requirement. While they have the best intentions, the road to a significant data breach is paved with the best intentions. No regulation or industry compliance advisory board will ever be able to keep up with the threat landscape. With that said, depending on your industry, you will most likely have to comply with something. It is important to focus on what you must do and separate that from what you should do.

If, for instance, you require some level of payment card industry data security standard (PCI DSS) compliance you will need a clean desk policy. If you aren't pursuing PCI certification there is no need to expend resources on creating a policy for the sake of creating a policy. This type of understanding will require knowledge of those laws and requirements, which is why hiring is so very important for security. These are just some of the industry-specific and national and state cybersecurity compliance standards and regulations, all of which have many books dedicated to that specific standard.

MASTER SERVICE AGREEMENTS, TERMS AND CONDITIONS, OH MY

Beyond regulatory or industry compliance you will also need to be compliant with the legal agreements you enter into with both customers and vendors. This is a process that you should always have legal counsel involved in, regardless of whether it's you and one other founder, or if you've just closed your A round of funding. When it comes to executing terms and conditions (T&Cs) or master service agreements (MSAs) you should first attempt to have these executed on your paper – meaning a document you've created, or your legal counsel has created, for your business.[1] This might not always be possible as you sell into larger and larger organizations that will most likely have their own legal contracts they want vendors to sign.

When pushed by a customer to sign on their paper you must seek advice from legal counsel. Things like liability, indemnification, termination clauses, and renewals, among others, will most likely be weighted completely in their favor and against your start-up. This is not something to take lightly, even if they are a lighthouse customer and you've known the executive buyer influencer (EBI) since grade school. This is purely a business transaction and should be approached as such.

These can be extraordinarily large documents and may have carve-outs, amendments, or addendums that specifically speak to cybersecurity requirements. It is critical to review the entire document with legal counsel and especially important to pay close attention to cybersecurity requirements. When reviewing these components of your agreement be on the lookout for the customer referencing specific technologies. This is where the customer inserts a requirement to use a specific piece of technology, or a specific vendor. You'll hopefully be closing deals with hundreds if not thousands of customers; these types of caveats will be impossible to track and comply with in the long run. You could even end up signing agreements that are in direct violation with each other. For example, if two different customers specify a different vendor to be used for vulnerability management, you can't possibly use both solutions. From a technical standpoint, that would be a nightmare to manage, put unnecessary resource load on your systems, and be a duplicative cost. Look for the following additional sections.

PATCH AND VULNERABILITY MANAGEMENT

This section may attempt to prescribe service level agreements (SLAs) when it comes to installing a patch for a vulnerability in a system or piece of software. These timelines are almost always unreasonably short and you must take into account current and future customer needs when it comes to downtime and maintenance windows, which are associated with patching most of the time.

Customers may also ask for notification when a specific criticality of vulnerability is discovered in the system. This should also be redlined, as it would not be feasible to notify every customer each time a vulnerability is discovered, because this is an inherent part of human-developed software and a regular part of the software development life cycle. Having your own vulnerability and patch management policy that stipulates patching times would be a reasonable mitigating control in place of this requirement.

ANTIVIRUS

This can be the most confusing of all. Traditional antivirus created in the 1980s and 1990s is mostly a thing of the past these days in corporate environments. This technology is now being replaced with endpoint detection and response (EDR) or endpoint protection platform (EPP), discussed in Chapter 4. Customers may simply dictate that some type of technology is installed on endpoints.

Some may specify servers and user endpoints. Others might differentiate between environments, such as productions, staging, test, and development. You may be constrained in those specific environments as to what products even support your specific operating systems. Making this section as generic as possible is recommended. Be prepared to discuss mitigating controls if you end up redlining the entire section.

AUDITING

You will find "right to audit" clauses in almost every agreement you enter into today. This serves as a warning to vendors that you should ensure you are compliant with the terms, or else. Many of these will provide the customer with an ability to terminate the contract without notice if an audit turns up negative findings.

Be prepared to spend some time on this section. Nearly every right to audit clause you come across will put the burden of cost of the audit on your business as the vendor. When it comes to cybersecurity audits this can be time-consuming and costly. You should never allow the customer to conduct the audit; it should always be performed by a reputable and mutually agreed-upon thirty-party vendor. Meaning the auditor should be known, their work should be verifiable, and both you and your customers must agree on the vendor to use.

Additionally, you should attempt to change the language so that the customer is responsible for all costs with the third-party audit vendor. Also, the customer should agree to pay either fixed fee or time and material costs from your company to support the audit. Audits can be extremely time-consuming for your team. If you are only a team of 100, you probably won't have an internal audit or governance, risk, and compliance (GRC) team that would be responsible for managing this audit.

That means engineers and individual contributors and managers will be pulled off work improving your product to help complete an audit. You may also find remediation time requirements in this section. On average, this is anywhere from 30–60 days in most contracts with US-based companies. These timelines vary on the criticality of the finding. It's typically recommended to remove numeric times and insert a "best-effort" statement.

INCIDENT RESPONSE

In the unfortunate event that your company suffers a data breach, you will need to notify your customers. These sections are almost identical across industries regardless of the size of the organization. These will spell out who you will need to contact, typically an email alias. This is an important contact that you should incorporate into your customer relationship management (CRM) solution for customer records once you've onboarded them.

If you are in the middle of a data breach, that is the wrong time to start looking for customer contact information. You should pay close attention to the time frames that will typically be in this section. Organizations may ask for unreasonably short notifications windows, such as "supplier will notify the company within 12 hours of an incident." Typically 72 hours is a reasonable time.

This is again where legal counsel can help with semantics, as you will want clear internal definitions of an incident and data breach because they are two different things. Customers may even ask for notification immediately on all cybersecurity incidents, but this simply is not possible for any organization to support and should typically be redlined (when we say redline in this case we are referring to striking an entire sentence or section from the contract).

Customers will also typically ask for specific information to be provided when they are notified. You'll want to make sure this is the same across all of your contracts, or as close as possible. This will allow for expedited notifications and allow either your customer success managers to reach out individually or you yourself as the founder to send a blind carbon copy (BCC) email to all of your customers directly.

Care should be taken as to what information you agree to share, especially if the contact method is via email. Prior to sending any data breach notification email, you should have that information reviewed by both legal counsel and a PR firm. It's best to do this prior to an incident and have a boilerplate created that is free of stress from a data breach event, which is not the optimal time to write an email that will be highly scrutinized.

 ## POLICIES AND CONTROLS

Customers may also specifically dictate standards, frameworks, and regulations in their cybersecurity addendums. This will be highly dependent on both the industry your company is in as well as the industry your customer is in. For example, if you will be processing credit cards on behalf of your customer, they will most likely stipulate in the contract that you must comply with PCI DSS.

This is appropriate to specify the actual control framework. If you won't process credit cards whatsoever, then removing something specific like PCI DSS would be appropriate. When possible it is best to insert "industry best practices" to enable your organization to choose the right controls and frameworks that are best for your company. However, in highly regulated industries like retail, finance, or healthcare, this will not be an option.

 ## CHANGE MANAGEMENT

Few customers may ask for long change management windows for notifications to changes. These can be very broad at times and if you are a software-as-a-service (SaaS) provider, nearly impossible to comply with, as change is the nature of SaaS. This section is highly dependent on the service or product you are offering.

It makes sense to attempt to redline this entire section if you are a SaaS provider. If you must keep it, shorter notification windows are more beneficial, typically, to your organization. Again, you hope to have thousands of customers; it would be nearly impossible to synchronize a change window across all of them in a single-tenant environment.

ENCRYPTION

Both data in motion (data being transferred from one system to another) and data at rest (data that is stored in a location) will most likely appear in some contractual agreements. This is especially true in the financial and healthcare industries.

It's best to avoid perspective controls, such as versions of types of encryption like transport layer security (TLS) version 1.2 or advanced encryption standard 256 (AES 256). TLS is the underlying protocol that encrypts web traffic: think of the hypertext transfer protocol secure (HTTPS) before a uniform resource locator (URL) in your browser. AES is a common standard for encrypting data at rest. Replacing these terms with more generic wording such as "industry standard" or "commercially available" allows for software to be updated as needed and prevents locking you into software or versions that may be insecure in the future and where an upgrade could possibly violate your agreement.

You may also come across the request to bring your own keys – "BYOK" – in these sections. Customers may want the ability to supply and control their own encryption keys for their specific data in your service. This is pretty rare and in most start-ups this might not be applicable at all. This will be something to review with your team depending on your product and service and could very well be a requirement. For example, if you are building an email encryption solution, a customer may rightfully ask to control those keys. This can also be a requirement for them to remain compliant with specific regulations.

DATA LOSS PREVENTION

Data loss prevention (DLP) is not an easy thing to implement, even in the most mature organizations. This clause is one you should push back on as hard as possible. You can mitigate striking it completely if there is a stipulation for data breach notifications. Saying you will prevent a data loss is nearly impossible and is signing you up for unreasonable liability.

 ## DATA PROCESSING AGREEMENT

As with the other topics discussed in this chapter, it is vital you engage legal counsel for this document as well. The Data Processing Agreement (DPA), as part of General Data Protection Regulation (GDPR), California Consumer Privacy Act (CCPA), and other privacy laws, is an agreement that you as the likely data processor and your customer as the data controller will enter into. For GDPR this is strictly for European Union (EU) citizen data. If you don't do business there or process any EU citizen data you might not have to worry about this. Additionally, as you may have already assumed, CCPA only applies to citizens of California.

It is important to note you will need a separate DPA for each. One does not cover all requirements.

The Data Processing Agreement is a rehashed and repackaged document of nearly all the same ubiquitous language we already see in terms and conditions today. But now that GDPR exists, everything is now relabeled and presented as net new. As the data processor, you will have limited leeway to redline anything in this document.

This does go both ways, so you could also incorporate your own DPA into contracts with vendors of yours, if you have EU citizen data.[1]

 ## SUMMARY

Compliance is not always lumped in with cybersecurity but it is important we cover the topic in this book. Privacy and legal work closely with and in some cases overlap with cybersecurity. In many cases you need cybersecurity in order to have privacy.

Having the appropriate counsel and advice when reviewing legal documents is important to all aspects of your start-up. And as we've seen, there can be many cybersecurity-related requirements in these legal agreements.

With both a legal expert and cybersecurity expert to advise on these documents you will be able to properly manage risk for your start-up.

 ACTION PLAN

- Work with general counsel or outside legal to build legal documents such as MSAs, T&Cs, and DPAs. Including languages and sections around security is great to state your terms up front instead of letting the customer propose them.
- If you have contracts already in place, review them for these security provisions with legal and cybersecurity advisors.
- If you will do business in the EU, look for recommendations on legal firms to use that are based in the EU. They can assist with GDPR, and some will also act as your data privacy officer (DPO). GDPR requires your DPO to be an EU citizen.

 NOTE

1. A template can be found on the helpful GDPR website, https://gdpr.eu/data-processing-agreement/.

CHAPTER TEN

Industry and Government Standards and Regulations

If you make ten thousand regulations you destroy all respect for the law.

– Winston Churchill

R EGULATIONS IS AN IMMENSE TOPIC and this chapter covers the most popular and widely known that impact cybersecurity for start-ups. Each of these topics have books dedicated to those specific frameworks, regulations, and laws. So as you read through this chapter and find those that are applicable to you I recommend reading more about that specific topic.

These are also the most common standards and regulations you will see referenced in terms and conditions, which we reviewed in Chapter 9. You should be aware of each of these and be familiar with any that are mentioned in legally binding contracts with customers, partners, etc.

OPEN SOURCE

OWASP

The Open Web Application Security Project® (OWASP) is a community that has created a set of standards for writing secure code. Every few years they publish a list, called the OWASP Top 10, of the top vulnerabilities in software; these are mostly web applications. This is an important standard to know and follow if you are building a software-as-a-service product or any type of web or mobile application. Most penetration testing firms will evaluate you based on this standard or you can ask that it be evaluated when negotiating your statement-of-work (SOW).

There is no specific certification a company can get for this standard. Figure 10.1 provides a description of each application risk in the OWASP Top 10 version 2017.

Center for Internet Security 20

The Center for Internet Security (CIS) is a non-profit that develops various controls and benchmarks to apply cybersecurity to systems and organizations. One of the more popular lists is the CIS Top 20, which is a list of critical controls they believe an organization should implement to achieve a sound cybersecurity program. This is another standard many firms can evaluate your company on and there is no certification you can receive for this. Figure 10.2 shows the different levels of CIS Top 20 and the controls within each of those levels.

UNITED STATES PUBLIC

SOC

Service Organization Controls (SOC) is a set of reports defined by the Statement on Standards for Attestation Engagements (SSAE) 16 standard created by the American Institute of Certified Public Accountants (AICPA). The SSAE 16 standard replaced the previous Statement on Auditing Standards (SAS) 70. There are three reports: SOC 1, dealing with financials; SOC 2, dealing with five specific trust principles; and SOC 3, a high-level report that is shareable publicly, unlike the SOC 2. Most organizations looking to both audit and report on their cybersecurity maturity will opt for SOC 2.

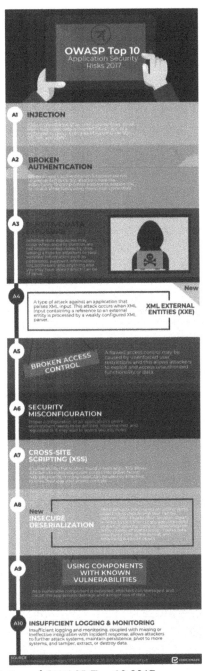

FIGURE 10.1 Depiction of OWASP Top 10 2017
Source: https://www.checkmarx.com/2017/11/30/infographic-owasp-top-10-
application-security-risks/

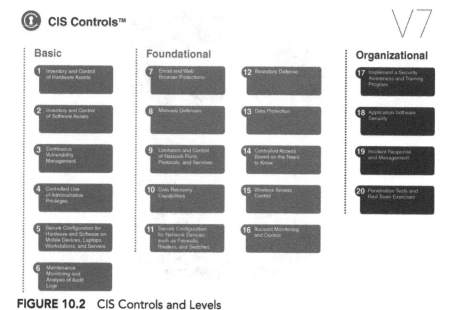

FIGURE 10.2 CIS Controls and Levels
Source: www.cisecurity.org

SOC 2 has two types of reports: a Type I that looks at a specific point in time, and Type II, which reviews the specific Trust Criteria you've selected over a specified date range. When scoping such an audit there are five Trust Criteria principles to select from:

Security
Availability
Processing integrity
Confidentiality
Privacy

Of these, privacy is the most complex and can add additional cost to such an audit. I recommend starting with SOC 2 Type I, with the smallest possible scope and security, availability, and confidentiality out of the five Trust Criteria principles. Figure 10.3 shows the different SOC report types, what is included, and who the typical user would be.

SOC Report Comparison

	WHAT IT REPORTS ON	WHO USES IT
SOC 1	Internal controls over financial reporting	User auditor and users' controller's office
SOC 2	Security, availability, processing integrity, confidentiality, or privacy controls	Shared under NDA by management, regulators, and others
SOC 3	Security, availability, processing integrity, confidentiality, or privacy controls	Publicly available to anyone

FIGURE 10.3   SOC Report Types Comparison
Source: https://www.otava.com/blog/soc-1-soc-2-soc-3-report-comparison/

 RETAIL

PCI DSS

Payment card industry data security standard (PCI DSS), or just PCI, is a standard created by the payment card industry in 2006 involving MasterCard, American Express, Visa, JCB International, and Discover Financial Services.

The PCI DSS organization has excellent resources available on their website.[1] You can find a significant amount of information here, far more than we will cover in this book. The PCI DSS website should be your first stop if this will be a requirement for your start-up.

PCI DSS is a requirement that you must comply with regardless of the number of credit cards you process. As this number goes up the requirements increase. There are four levels to PCI, with level 1 being the highest if you process over 6 million credit cards per year. As a start-up, you may only process a small fraction of this and could possibly complete a self-assessment questionnaire in which there are several different types. If your company operates in fintech and you anticipate processing high volumes of credit cards you will most likely need to engage a third-party auditor.

A PCI audit should result in a record of compliance (ROC, pronounced "rock"). This audit is done by an auditor approved by the PCI Security Standards Council. You can find a list of these auditors on the PCI security standards website. You can expect to pay anywhere from $30,000 to well over $250,000 depending on the auditing firm you choose. The prestige and notoriety of the auditor will often dictate the higher costs.

You may ask, how do I know what auditor to select? If you are trying to win lighthouse customers that put significant stock into who your auditor is, you may need to go with a tier 1 or "big 4" auditor. If you've been through a PCI audit already, and have established customers, using a tier 2 or tier 3 auditor may be more cost-effective and achieve the same result of compliance. Remember, some customers may want to conduct their own third-party audit regardless of your legitimate and industry-approved audit and ROC.

SAQ A – Card-not-Present Merchants, All Cardholder Data Functions Fully Outsourced

SAQ A-EP – Partially Outsourced E-Commerce Merchants Using a Third-Party Website for Payment Processing

SAQ B – Merchants with Only Imprint Machines or Only Standalone, Dial-Out Terminals, No Electronic Cardholder Data Storage

SAQ B-IP – Merchants with Standalone, IP-Connected PTS Point-of-Interaction (POI) terminals, No Electronic Cardholder Data Storage

SAQ C-VT – Merchants with Web-Based Virtual Terminals, No Electronic Cardholder Data Storage

SAQ C – Merchants with Payment Application Systems Connected to the Internet, No Electronic Cardholder Data Storage

SAQ P2PE – Merchants Using Only Hardware Payment Terminals in a PCI SSC-listed P2PE Solution, No Electronic Cardholder Data Storage

SAQ D for Merchants – All Other SAQ-Eligible Merchants

SAQ D for Service Providers – SAQ-Eligible Service Providers

PCI is updated regularly and frequently and it is recommended to review the PCI standards website for the latest compliance information.

If you are going to process credit cards you will need to be compliant with PCI DSS.

Depending on your customers you may need to be audited by an independent party against the PCI DSS standards to obtain a ROC that a customer may require. This situation is typically found in business-to-business (B2B) industries. A converse example would be a company like Square, which is marketed direct to consumers, mostly small businesses who won't demand to see a ROC, but Square must work with credit card issuers and payment processes who will require that the PCI standard is followed and audited.

SOX

The Sarbanes-Oxley Act of 2002 (SOX)[2] applies to publicly held American companies. SOX was sponsored by Sen. Paul Sarbanes (D-MD) and Rep. Michael G. Oxley (R-OH-4) and signed into law in 2002. SOX is important to understand and eventually prepare for when you plan to IPO. SOX is not a requirement for privately held start-ups, yet this should be on your radar. In the law there are two sections that specifically mention information security even though the law is designed to increase the financial reporting of public companies.

While not specifically cybersecurity related you should consider getting an initial public offering (IPO) readiness assessment anywhere from two to three years before your planned IPO. Most major auditing firms can conduct these assessments for you.[3]

ENERGY, OIL, AND GAS

The energy sector is highly regulated for many obvious reasons. The dangerous nature of working with large volumes of highly volatile resources requires strong standards. Now that the digital world has found new and innovative solutions for this industry, many of these systems are now being connected to the Internet. This has prompted regulators to develop new standards on protecting these unique systems when it comes to cybersecurity.

NERC CIP

The North American Electric Reliability Corporation (NERC) created the Critical Infrastructure Protection (CIP) set of standards[4] in 2003, which were then voluntary and are now mandatory for bulk power systems as well as vendors that service this industry. In 2016, the Federal Energy Regulatory Commission in the United States changed CIP to now cover vendors to the energy industry; this change went into effect in 2020.[5]

The set of CIP controls covers 15 individual domains. NERC conducts all audits, so it is not something like PCI where you'd initiate an audit and receive a certification at the end of it. A NERC audit may happen any time after 30 days from notification. A periodic audit may happen about once every three years.[6]

ISA-62443-3-3 (99.03.03)-2013

The International Society of Automation (ISA) is a non-profit that develops standards around automating industry control systems.[7] ANSI/ISA-62443-3-3 (99.03.03)-2013 is Security for Industrial Automation and Control Systems: System Security Requirements and Security Levels. This is part of ISA-62443,[8] which is non-regulated and provides a framework for the security of industrial control systems as well as Internet of Things (IoT).

Federal Energy Regulatory Commission

The Federal Energy Regulatory Commission (FERC) regulates the transmission of electricity and natural gas in the United States. FERC also oversees the North American Electric Reliability Corporation (NERC).

Department of Energy Cybersecurity Framework

The United States Department of Energy developed a Cybersecurity Framework, which has created a maturity model called the Cybersecurity Capabilities Maturity Model (C2M2).[9] This was specifically designed for the energy sector and there are now models for the energy subsector (ES-C2M2) and oil and natural gas (ONG-C2M2). While not a certification, it provides a framework to measure the maturity of your organization's cybersecurity. This model covers 10 domains with a maturity indicator level (MIL) from zero to three, three being the highest possible level.

The C2M2 can be self-facilitated; however, there are some firms that can conduct this assessment for a fee. While there is no certification to provide this, it can produce additional evidential documentation to provide to customers if your start-up targets companies in this sector. Having a C2M2 is not necessarily a requirement, legal or otherwise, but may show up in the contracting process.

HEALTH

Like the energy sector, healthcare is also highly regulated. From patient treatment to pharmaceuticals, there is nothing that the government doesn't touch. There are both laws and industry-created standards that organizations must follow. As the value of health data continues to rise, so does the frequency and impact of data breaches around health data. From health insurance providers to family practices, these are all prime targets for this valuable data that typically has a long shelf life[10] and attackers are willing to pay for on the dark web.

HIPAA

Health Insurance Portability and Accountability Act (HIPAA) is a US government law and regulation that stipulates cybersecurity protections for health data. Anyone with health data must comply with HIPAA. However, there is no certification to obtain or to become compliant with. HIPAA is enforced by the Office for Civil Rights (OCR) within the United States Health and Human Services (HHS). This should not be confused with the more well-known Office for Civil Rights within the United States Department of Education.

Since there is no certification to obtain it is difficult to know if you are in compliance. Because OCR has the final say and only becomes involved after a complaint or incident, they will hold the final determination as to whether you were ultimately compliant. Several firms do offer assessment services based on HIPAA and their knowledge of publicly available OCR fines and enforcements. These should cost somewhere between $20,000 and $100,000 depending on the size of your organization and the scope of the assessment.

HHS also provides a self-assessment kit, the HIPAA Security Risk Assessment Tool, available on their website.[11] The National Institute of Standard and Technology (NIST) also has a self-assessment toolkit available, the NIST HIPAA Security Toolkit Application.[12] Both of these can be used to determine your level of compliance with HIPAA.

HITECH

The Health Information Technology for Economic and Clinical Health (HITECH) Act of 2009 stimulates the implementation of electronic health records.[13] It also expanded the protections of HIPAA from 1996. The HITECH Act adds additional breach notification requirements to HIPAA, provides funding for additional audits by federal agencies, and increases enforcement as well as maximum allowed fines.

HITRUST

The HITRUST Alliance or HITRUST (Health Information Trust Alliance) is a privately held organization that is made up of healthcare, technology, and cybersecurity organizations.[14] This alliance was formed to create the Common Security Framework (CSF) specifically for the healthcare industry.[15] The HITRUST CSF is a framework an organization can become certified by. HITRUST, like other frameworks, is conveniently mapped to other standards such as NIST CSF and ISO 27001, so compliance and certification of one greatly prepares your organization for the other.

 FINANCIAL

The financial sector rounds out the "big 3" when it comes to highly regulated industries. Like the others, many of the regulations spun out of huge disasters attempting to prevent black swans; as Milton Friedman says, there is nothing more permanent than a temporary government program.

FFIEC

Federal Financial Institutions Examination Council (FFIEC) is a body of five banking regulators in the United States that includes the Federal Reserve Board of Governors (FRB), the Federal Deposit Insurance

Corporation (FDIC), the National Credit Union Administration (NCUA), the Office of the Comptroller of the Currency (OCC), and the Consumer Financial Protection Bureau (CFPB).

In 2017, the FFIEC developed and published their own Cybersecurity Assessment tool that financial institutions can use to determine risks in their cybersecurity preparedness.[16]

FINRA

Financial Institutions Regulatory and Interest Rate Control Act of 1978 (FINRA) is the law that created FFIEC.

FINRA is also a government-authorized not-for-profit organization that oversees U.S. broker-dealers. They have also published a Small Firm Cybersecurity Checklist[17] specifically for small financial firms.

NCUA

The National Credit Union Administration (NCUA) sets standards for United States credit unions, to include cybersecurity controls, which they are audited on annually. The NCUA is one of the five banking regulators that make up the FFIEC. They, too, have their own specific guidance, tools, and resources for credit unions in the United States.[18]

EDUCATION

While also a regulated industry in the United States, education is not nearly as scrutinized as the energy, health, or finance sectors. The laws around both K12 and higher education don't really stipulate any cybersecurity requirements at all.

FERPA

The Family Educational Rights and Privacy Act of 1974 (FERPA) does not necessarily have specific cybersecurity controls stated in the law; however, it is worth mentioning since privacy is such a hot topic and overlaps significantly with cybersecurity. In order to have privacy, you must have cybersecurity.

INTERNATIONAL

Of course, most start-ups will eventually sell outside of their home country, how else do you get to the total addressable market (TAM)? This is another area where things can get very complicated very quickly. For example, European countries might all subscribe to GDPR but many have their own laws governing privacy and cybersecurity. It's best to work with general counsel to understand a specific country before targeting sales there.

International Organization for Standardization (ISO)

ISO[19] produced many globally accepted standards for many industries. Everything from manufacturing of physical goods to risk management to cybersecurity. The most well-known cybersecurity standard from ISO is the 27001 series, referred to as ISO 27001.[20] The accompanying standards specifications, ISO 27002, defines the standards for an organization's Information Security Management System. There are 14 control families that make up the standard, and to be certified you must show compliance in all of them.

There are many organizations that can conduct some or all parts of the ISO 27001 certification. However, the only organizations that can provide the final certification are ISO-certified registrars. The audit consists of two individual stages not including a gap assessment. When pursuing the ISO 27001 certification for the first time I highly recommend conducting a gap assessment first. A gap assessment will help you to evaluate your readiness for the stage 1 and stage 2 audits to achieve certifications. Because there are time limits to these audits, the gap assessment gives you insights into non-conformities and then you have more time to remediate. If you discover these during a stage 1, you may not have enough time to remediate those non-conformities, especially if they are deemed major.

The gap assessment will give you a first pass to understand where your organization stands. Once you schedule your stage 1 and stage 2 audits there is very little time in between to fix any findings that come out of stage 1. Conducting a gap assessment will provide more time to resolve any issues that are found.

You can expect an ISO 27001 to last no less than 4 months from start to finish and should take no more than 10 months. An ISO gap assessment may cost anywhere from $15,000 to $50,000. Your stage 1 and stage 2 audits to obtain certification can range from $20,000 to well over $100,000. Factors such as company size, the number of locations that are in scope, and the number of systems in scope will increase the cost.

UL 2900

Underwriters Laboratories (UL) certifies products for their safety. The UL 2900[21] series standard provides certification for a variety of Internet of Things, medical devices, and other control systems. This also pulls from the IEC 62443[22] standard. The certification for UL 2900 is provided under UL's Cybersecurity Assurance Program (CAP).[23]

This standard and certification is very applicable to any start-up founder that is building a consumer IoT product, smart home device, medical device, or other type of industry control system.

GDPR

General Data Protection Regulation (GDPR)[24] was approved in 2014 and replaces the European Data Protection Directive from 1995. GDPR became enforceable from May 2018 onward. GDPR covers citizens of the European Union and provides data privacy rights for their individual personal data. There are many components to GDPR and, as with any law and legal regulation, you should consult with your general or outside counsel to make sure you are compliant, if necessary. There is no exception, regardless if you are a start-up, to be compliant with GDPR.

Common items you will encounter with GDPR is the requirement for a Data Protection Officer (DPO)[25] who must be a European Union citizen. It is recommended that as a start-up you use outside counsel located in the EU as your DPO. You may consider hiring a DPO most likely after the growth phase. You will also most likely see data processing agreements (DPAs)[26] added to your terms and conditions when selling to customers in the EU if you are a business-to-business (B2B) start-up. DPAs were discussed in Chapter 9.

Privacy Shield

The EU–U.S. Privacy Shield framework replaced the International Safe Harbor Privacy Principles in 2015. However, since then Privacy Shield was also invalidated by the European Court of Justice in 2020. More information regarding this case is available by searching Schrems II.[27]

UK Cyber Essentials

The UK Cyber Essentials, basic and plus, is a certification that you can obtain from the UK National Cyber Security Centre.[28] This is sometimes a requirement for doing business with UK government agencies. In order to become Cyber Essentials Plus certified you must first become Cyber Essentials Basic certified. There are many vendors that have been accredited to conduct this certification and you'll need to engage with one to do either certification. These vendors are available via the IASME Consortium website.[29]

Once you've selected a vendor, they will provide access to a 40-question self-assessment. You can receive basic certification after completing this self-assessment. Once that is complete, there are a series of technical tests that the vendor will conduct to certify your start-up at the plus level. This includes having you install a vulnerability scanner on one of your user systems and allowing them to scan for vulnerabilities. If possible, I recommend providing a scan report if you are already using a vulnerability scanner and avoid installing unknown software. The vendor will also send test phishing emails to users to select, in order to see what is delivered to their inbox and if they open them. The part I find most interesting in this certification is they do no testing of your product. Your cloud infrastructure provider, such as AWS or Azure, is out of scope.

If you already have ISO 27001, it is highly recommended that you use this certification in lieu of the testing to receive plus certification.

 UNITED STATES FEDERAL AND STATE GOVERNMENT

Much of what we have discussed in this chapter is industry-specific US government laws and regulations. Many of these pull their standards from or directly reference many of the following standards.

NIST

The National Institute of Standards and Technology[30] is a non-regulatory agency and part of the United States Department of Commerce. Non-regulatory means that NIST does not create laws, but their standards are certainly referenced or included in many of the previous laws and regulations we have discussed in this chapter.

NIST has created hundreds of well-adopted standards since their founding in 1901 and today is one of the leading organizations creating cybersecurity standards. As a founder it is worth your valuable time to become familiar with the NIST Cybersecurity Framework (CSF).[31] The commonsense approach of this framework has led to fast adoption across many industries and by many cybersecurity vendors looking to align their products to this framework. Figure 10.4 describes the high-level components of the NIST Cybersecurity Framework's five pillars.

There are a number of great resources available on NIST's website and YouTube. There is a fantastic YouTube channel from Side Channel

NIST Cybersecurity Framework

IDENTIFY	PROTECT	DETECT	RESPOND	RECOVER
Asset management	Awareness control	Anomolies and events	Response Planning	Recover planning
Business environment	Awareness and training		Communications	
Governance	Data security	Security continuous monitoring	Analysis	Improvements
Risk assessment	Info protection and procedures		Mitigation	
Risk management strategy	Maintenance	Detection process	Improvements	Communications
	Protective technology			

FIGURE 10.4 NIST Cybersecurity Framework Pillars
Source: https://www.securityinfowatch.com/security-executives/security-industry-services/article/12427483/cybersecurity-assessments-an-overview

Security[32] creating quick videos about all components of NIST CSF that are easy to consume and understand.

NISPOM

The National Industrial Security Program Operating Manual (NISPOM) (DoD 5220.22-M)[33] is mostly applicable to federal defense contractors or cleared defense contractors (CDC). The Defense Counterintelligence and Security Agency is the governing body for the National Industrial Security Program, which was established by Executive Order 12829. NISPOM focuses on insider threat and protecting cleared defense contractors from those threats.

DFARS PGI

The Defense Federal Acquisition Regulation Supplement (DFARS), Procedures, Guidance, and Information (PGI)[34] is the organization that sets standards for how the Department of Defense makes purchases. There are many standards that cover nearly everything you can think of, including cybersecurity. If you are planning to bid on government contracts you can expect to see these requirements in your request for proposals (RFP). You will definitely want to consult with general counsel familiar with government contracts.

FedRAMP

FedRAMP is an endeavor in and of itself. This is specifically for organizations that sell directly to the United States government. It is a complex, expensive, and time-consuming process that may not always yield desired results (closing big government contracts and increasing revenue or ACV). FedRAMP has an excellent website that provides high-level details and granular specifications on obtaining this certification.[35]

FedRAMP consists of three levels that you can be certified at: low, medium, and high. It's no surprise that most go for medium. You will also need to engage approved third-party assessment organizations (3PAOs), one for the advisory phase, and one for the assessment phase. The vendors cannot be the same.

You will also need a federal agency to sponsor your business for the certification. However, you don't need to be sponsored to start the advisory or assessment phases. When selecting a 3PAO, an experienced firm can be incredibly helpful in the advisory portion, as they can help guide you and also recommend agencies whose FedRAMP teams are best suited to your business.

When reviewing 3PAOs you may find many that can do either advisory or assessment work and some that only do assessments. You may find with firms that can do both that they will push to do the assessment work. That is because the continuous monitoring (ConMon) requirement of FedRAMP precludes the firm that does the advisory work from the follow-on continuous monitoring for a one-year period. And once you are locked in with a vendor that does your assessment and then will do your continuous monitoring, it doesn't make a lot of sense to switch.

Every federal agency has its own FedRAMP team, whose skills and experience vary. Getting the right sponsoring agency is important to the long-term success of your FedRAMP status. A long list of approved 3PAOs is available on the FedRAMP marketplace and all businesses that have some FedRAMP status, agencies that are customers of that business, and who their sponsor is.

You can expect the process to take a year from start to receiving certification status and cost anywhere from $300,000 to $500,000 just for 3PAO services. Figure 10.5 shows the joint authorization board workflow

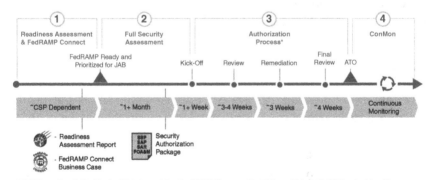

FIGURE 10.5 Joint Authorization Board (JAB) Workflow
Source: www.fedramp.gov

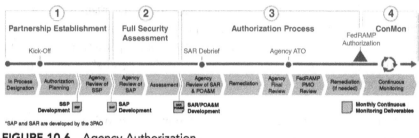

FIGURE 10.6 Agency Authorization
Source: www.fedramp.gov

for FedRAMP approval. Figure 10.6 shows the agency authorization work-flow for FedRAMP.

FISMA

The Federal Information Security Management Act of 2002 is the law that gives NIST the authority to create standards that government agencies must adhere to.

NYCRR 500

New York state passed 23 NYCRR Part 500 into law and subsequently became effective in 2017 for specific cybersecurity controls of financial institutions.[36] There are a great number of exemptions for covered entities and if your start-up is in the financial sector and in New York you should review these requirements. An interesting and widely discussed component of this law is the requirement to hire a chief information security officer (CISO) if you qualify as a covered entity.

CCPA

The California Consumer Privacy Act (CCPA) is the state of California's hyper-localized answer to General Data Protection Regulation (GDPR). CCPA provides additional rights to citizens of California and their control over their data. Most commonly is CCPA requests that allow consumers to request a company to provide a copy of their data, which the company holds. Like GDPR, it provides the option to ask that your data is removed. Understanding what standards you may be held accountable to will help inform your cybersecurity strategy and roadmap.

SUMMARY

Laws and regulations are daunting. For better or for worse, we must address them as a business risk. And there is no end in sight of new laws regulating cybersecurity. GDPR won't be the last big privacy and cybersecurity law. This by far is one area worth spending the resources to work with general counsel, inside or outside, to fully understand your start-up's liabilities and requirements.

Understanding what you must be compliant with versus what you can push back on, carve out, or just completely ignore, will greatly help to define your cybersecurity roadmap and strategy, which we talk about in the next chapter.

Thankfully, many if not all of these standards greatly overlap. Many industries attempt to develop their own set of standards to give the appearance, as an industry, that they are doing their due diligence when it comes to cybersecurity. The list seems daunting but you should not be overwhelmed. These standards and regulations are requirements.

However, before investing in checking the box and becoming compliant, the best foundational place to start is with CIS Critical Security Controls. These specific technical controls are mapped to nearly every other major standard or framework currently in use. This framework is what provides the foundation knowledge for this book.

As I mentioned earlier, this book is about scaling security with your start-up. Many of the controls in the CIS Critical Security Controls, as well as the compliance and regulation standards I mentioned, are unnecessary for almost every start-up. There are 20 total overall control families in the list and you should follow at least 5 of the 20 from day one.

ACTION PLAN

- Define what industries you will either operate in or sell into.
- Review the relevant regulations with general counsel to determine what you must comply with.
- Review the necessary applicable regulations to incorporate those standards into your cybersecurity roadmap and strategy.

- If you have not yet hired internal general counsel or outside counsel, now is the time to do so.
- Go back to Chapter 2 and your roadmap document and add specific standards applicable to your start-up to your roadmap document.

NOTES

1. https://www.pcisecuritystandards.org/
2. https://www.congress.gov/bill/107th-congress/house-bill/3763
3. https://www.ey.com/en_us/ipo/readiness-assessment;
   https://www.pwc.com/mn/en/capital-markets/roadmap-for-an-ipo
   .html;
   https://advisory.kpmg.us/services/corporate-strategy-mergers-
   acquisitions/mergers-acquisitions/accounting-advisory-services/
   ipo-readiness.html
4. https://www.nerc.com/pa/Stand/Pages/CIPStandards.aspx
5. https://www.ferc.gov/sites/default/files/2020-04/E-2_9.pdf
6. https://www.powermag.com/preparing-for-a-nerc-cip-audit/;
   https://blog.rsisecurity.com/nerc-cip-standards-what-you-need-to-
   know/;
   https://www.nerc.com/pa/comp/Documents/Supply_Chain_Cyber_
   Security_Practices_20190306.pdf.
7. https://www.isa.org/products/ansi-isa-62443-3-3-99-03-03-
   2013-security-for-indu
8. https://www.tripwire.com/state-of-security/regulatory-compliance/
   isa-iec-62443-framework/
9. https://www.energy.gov/ceser/activities/cybersecurity-critical-
   energy-infrastructure/energy-sector-cybersecurity-0
10. Health data is typically immutable (it doesn't change) and remains valid sometimes as long as a person's life. This is unlike credit card data that has an expiration data and typically becomes invalid after its first malicious use.
11. https://www.healthit.gov/topic/privacy-security-and-hipaa/
    security-risk-assessment-tool
12. https://csrc.nist.gov/projects/security-content-automation-protocol/
    hipaa

13. https://www.hhs.gov/hipaa/for-professionals/special-topics/hitech-act-enforcement-interim-final-rule/index.html

14. https://hitrustalliance.net/

15. https://hitrustalliance.net/hitrust-csf/

16. https://www.ffiec.gov/cyberassessmenttool.htm

17. https://www.finra.org/compliance-tools/cybersecurity-checklist

18. https://www.ncua.gov/regulation-supervision/regulatory-compliance-resources/cybersecurity-resources

19. Yes, the name of the organization is International Organization of Standardization and is called ISO not IOS.

20. https://www.iso.org/isoiec-27001-information-security.html

21. https://www.ul.com/offerings/cybersecurity-assurance-and-compliance

22. https://www.isa.org/training-and-certification/isa-certification/isa99iec-62443/isa99iec-62443-cybersecurity-certificate-programs

23. https://www.ul.com/resources/ul-cybersecurity-assurance-program-ul-cap

24. https://gdpr.eu/

25. https://gdpr.eu/data-protection-officer/

26. https://gdpr.eu/what-is-data-processing-agreement/

27. https://www.roythorne.co.uk/site/blog/corporate-and-commercial-blog/Schrems-II-explained-in-a-nutshell

28. https://www.ncsc.gov.uk/cyberessentials/overview

29. https://iasme.co.uk/cyber-essentials/

30. https://www.nist.gov/

31. https://www.nist.gov/cyberframework

32. https://www.youtube.com/c/sidechannel

33. https://www.dcsa.mil/mc/ctp/nisp/

34. https://www.acq.osd.mil/DPAP/dars/dfarspgi/current/index.html

35. https://www.fedramp.gov

36. https://www.dfs.ny.gov/industry_guidance/cyber_faqs

CHAPTER ELEVEN

Communicating Your Cybersecurity Posture and Maturity to Customers

Practice isn't the thing you do once you're good. It's the thing you do that makes you good.

– Malcolm Gladwell

USTOMERS WILL CONTINUE TO BECOME more risk-averse when it comes to the vendors they do business with and trust with their data. Just like in high school, showing your work is still important. Customers want evidence that you are meeting minimum requirements. This can be helpful to sales – but can also bring them to a grinding halt.

Your sales team should be generally familiar with your cybersecurity program and practices. If you have certifications like SOC2 or PCI DSS, they should be capable of talking about these at a high level with customers. When the customers dig in, the sales lead should know who to bring into the conversation to make the customer feel comfortable. While sales operations is a huge topic unto itself and there are many books on this, it is important we cover cybersecurity in the sales process.

Discussing it up front in the first pitch with a customer is important; a single slide just mentioning cybersecurity at your company and how it is baked into the culture and product go a long way. Be up front and transparent. These details obviously will shift and change as you grow. Selling to your first lighthouse customers[1] may not require as much high touch transparency on cybersecurity, but certainly, for future customers it will. Make sure how you talk about how cybersecurity in your sales process matures with how you talk about your product.

Understanding who you are selling to is always critical. Who is your buyer in the organization, what is their level, do they influence the business, are they an individual contributor or executive? These will be significant factors in getting through various vendor review processes. While you might be selling to one individual in the organization, you must also sell to their finance team, legal team, procurement team, cybersecurity team, and privacy team.

If you have no certifications or evidence to provide, you will most likely be stuck having to complete a vendor cybersecurity questionnaire. These can range in length, complexity, and intrusiveness, based on the sector your product is in and the vertical your customer is in.

CERTIFICATIONS AND AUDITS

Certifications and audits can provide a view into your start-up's cybersecurity maturity. They can also instill confidence in your customers, partners, and employees that cybersecurity is a priority for your start-up. In Chapter 10 we discussed a handful of various regulations, laws, and

FIGURE 11.1   Popular Certification Control Coverage Robustness
Source: https://www.complianceforge.com/nist-sp-800-53-r4-r5-policies-standards-procedures/

standards that are applicable to different industries and business types. The two that can be applied to nearly any start-up, regardless of the type of business, is SOC2 and ISO 27001. You can read more about these in Chapter 10. Figure 11.1 shows a comparison of popular certifications and frameworks based on their control family coverage.

QUESTIONNAIRES

Shared Assessments

The Shared Assessments Program[2] produces an annual update to the Standard Information Gathering questionnaire, also called the "SIG." This document, which is usually provided in Excel format, covers 18 topic domains and ranges from 300 to 1600 questions depending on the version that is used. There is also the SIG Lite, which has the least questions and SIG Full, which has all questions. There is an annual license associated with this document and it is a good starting point if you don't have an industry certification like SOC2, ISO 27001, or PCI DSS. It is also significantly less expensive than obtaining one of these certifications. While it does not replace a reputable third-party auditor it can help show customers your cybersecurity maturity. Figure 11.2 shows the Shared Assessments third-party risk management workflow.

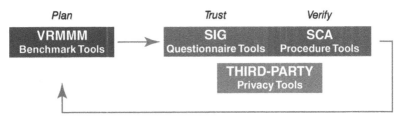

FIGURE 11.2   Shared Assessments Third-Party Risk Management Toolkit Workflow

Source: https://sharedassessments.org/blog/2020-tprm-toolkit-announce/

Cloud Security Alliance

The Cloud Security Alliance[3] is another organization that produces the Consensus Assessment Initiative Questionnaire (CIAQ, pronounced "cake"), which also comes in different versions. This is also an Excel document with a variety of questions you answer "yes" or "no" to and provide additional commentary. There is currently no cost associated with downloading a copy of this questionnaire. It does not go as in-depth as the SIG but provides an excellent window into your company's cybersecurity maturity, especially if you are a SaaS product built in a cloud environment.

The Cloud Security Alliance has also created the security trust assurance and risk (STAR), which is a set of controls that an organization can be audited against and then certified at five different levels. Figure 11.3 shows the Cloud Security Alliance STAR certification levels by comparison.

Vendor Security Alliance

The Vendor Security Alliance (VSA)[4] also provides a free questionnaire in both a short and long version, the VSA-Full and VSA-Core. Like the SIG and CIAQ, it also addresses privacy concerns like CCPA and GDPR. This is also provided in an Excel document that you can download from their website. VSA also offers the ability to make your completed questionnaire part of a repository that customers can buy a subscription to and then review your document via their portal.

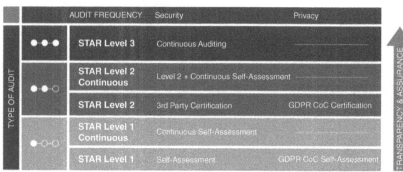

FIGURE 11.3 CSA STAR Levels
Source: https://cloudsecurityalliance.org/star/

You can expect customers to use these questionnaires or customize them to attempt to determine the level of risk when onboarding a vendor. This is why it is so important to ensure everyone you sell to at an organization understands exactly what they are buying. Many times the vendor review process at a company is not applicable to your product in any way.

When you get to the stage in the sales cycle where you are either about to start a proof of value (POV) or start negotiating terms, it is very valuable to have a single page at the top of your terms and conditions (Ts and Cs) or master service agreement (MSA) that describes what they are buying, in plain language, free of jargon or buzzwords, and includes a statement about cybersecurity.

This will help as the document flows through the customer's processes, and each individual who must sign off on it can quickly understand what it is they are buying and why no additional reviews are necessary. This can prevent costly delays in the sales cycle. If the process has to stop and that business owner – for example, your customer's general counsel – now needs to go back to your customer (the person buying your product) and ask them to explain the product, it could bring up more questions. Then your customer has to reach out to your sales team with new questions; if that account executive doesn't have those answers, they now need to find the right person in your organization to answer them.

Anticipate questions up front. This is something your board of advisors, investors, or other key advisors can help you tabletop and figure out what questions might come up from various individuals in your target companies. And as you sell into large and larger organizations, the questions will grow exponentially.

SHARING DATA WITH YOUR CUSTOMER

Before sharing any sensitive data I highly recommend you have the requesting party execute a non-disclosure agreement (NDA) When it comes to sharing any data externally about your cybersecurity program you want to make sure that your communications and legal representatives are involved. You want to make sure the data you share maintains your narrative and also does not conflict with any customer contracts. The last thing you want to do is to proactively share data about your cybersecurity program and in turn create a liability with a customer, prospect, partner, employees, or investors.

Once you have one or more of the items we've discussed so far in this chapter, such as a certification, audit report, or industry questionnaire, you should consider a security page on your website. This is typically something like security.your-unicorn-startup.com or www.your-unicorn-startup .com/security. This is very common to find today and is quickly becoming the standard. An excellent example of this would be the secure messaging app Wickr, https://wickr.com/security/. They have a comprehensive and very transparent security page.

These can be self-hosted or there are many vendors that offer this type of service, typically called third-party risk management (TPRM). Having some type of security page to show you are even thinking about it is the first step. Then when customers ask for proof, having evidence like certifications, audits, penetration test reports, questionnaires, and white papers will back up those claims.

Again, before sharing these documents you should have an NDA in place. When it comes to audits and certifications these can easily be protected with adding a passphrase to encrypt the file; both Microsoft Word and Adobe Acrobat allow you to protect files in this way. You'll also want to have a password manager in place so you can store the passphrase you've used to protect that file. I would also recommend a different passphrase for each time you share the documents with a new client. This adds to the control you have over the file, so then only the intended company can open it. Lastly, you may consider adding a watermark to the file with the customer name, email address of your contact at that customer, and the date you shared it. If you do add this, you will want to set a separate passphrase for editing the document. If you omit this, anyone that can open the file could edit it and remove the watermark.

This process can become time consuming if you have many customers requesting these cybersecurity documents, so it can be very valuable to use a TPRM vendor to streamline this process and host the files for you. Many can automatically do many of the steps we just discussed with a single click. These TPRM vendors can even provide a click-through NDA so you don't even have to manage getting the customer to sign your NDA before accessing the documents.

Completing one of the questionnaires we cover in this chapter is also a great way to provide these key details to customers. The customers that do use these standard forms can then take your completed document and load it easily into their own vendor management system. This helps to enable sales and streamline the sales process on both sides.

Technical documents like penetration tests should also be strongly protected. Typically, a start-up would only share what is called the executive summary with a customer. This is a high-level description of the scope of the penetration test and key findings. I would not recommend sharing the entire report unless you accompany it with a detailed remediation document where you have addressed all the findings in the report.

CASE STUDY

Sam, Jess, and Michael founded their sales enablement start-up 100X eighteen months ago and have just over $1MM in annual recurring revenue (ARR). Their software-as-a-service (SaaS) platform allows sales leaders to supercharge their teams by bringing together data from disparate sales tools, leading to faster deal cycles and increased deal sizes.

They've done very well with two massive lighthouse customers and many other early stage start-ups. They are now pushing into large Fortune 1000 enterprises with longer and more complex deal cycles. Their sales team keeps getting blindsided by last-minute security and privacy reviews from these customers and sending these questions to the executive team to help answer. To get full value out of the platform. customers must allow access to their own sensitive sales data, and the cybersecurity teams in these customer organizations need to have a lot of probing questions.

They already have SOC2 Type I certification because the board member that introduced them to one of the lighthouse customers said they needed it. But beyond that, there is no other documentation about how 100X handles customer privacy. Jess contacts a friend who is the CEO at an alumni start-up and who also came out of the same start-up accelerator as 100X. That founder shares with Jess similar hurdles they overcame and gives Jess some action items.

The 100X executive staff decides in their weekly meeting that they'll have the design firm that built their website add a "/security" page to the site that shows off their certifications and talks about how they encrypt user data and other controls they have in place. The go-to market (GTM) team also adds a slide to the standard sales pitch deck that summarizes what is on the website.

After a month of adding these low-cost items to the sales cycle there has been a 75% reduction in the amount of cybersecurity reviews the sales team is being asked to complete by prospects. However, several sales teams are reporting even more intrusive questions about privacy, GDPR, and CCPA. Prospects are sending long documents containing both technical questions and questions that don't seem to be applicable to their platform.

Sam, Jess, and Michael meet with the rest of the executive team again. They actually lost a $175,000 deal because the customer's procurement team rejected 100X as a vendor, based on the responses to the questionnaire document they sent over. It turns out the account executive, in an attempt to close the deal eight days before the end of quarter, completed the answers themselves. Because the account executive (AE) did not have all the correct information, the answers were incomplete, wrong, or incoherent. This was a red flag for the prospect customer's risk team reviewing 100X as a vendor and stopped the deal from moving forward. Sam, Jess, and Michael realized they had to act quickly.

The entire executive team conducted a lesson learned on the deal with that sales manager and then reviewed each question in the document provided by the prospect. They spent five hours answering all 388 questions in that document and used it as a template for the rest of the sales team going forward. The answers were saved in the central sales material folder so all account executives could access the information at any time and provide the correct answer each time.

In the last 12 months since implementing the knowledge repository for the sales teams, 100X has not lost a single deal to issues in the prospect customer's procurement cycle. The number of cybersecurity questionnaires they are asked to complete has been reduced by 37%. This is because the sales team can instantaneously share those 388 answers when there is any question about 100X's cybersecurity program. The team is now faced with a different problem, as they have increased all AEs' books of business but have not been adding additional sales reps to the teams. This means that what was a manageable manual process for each AE to handle cybersecurity questions from customers then became more difficult as the workload increased. This has again had a negative effect on deal-closing timelines.

Sam goes back through her emails from the last year and finds several cold sales emails from third-party risk management vendors. After many discovery and demo calls with 12 vendors in this space, the executive team decides to go with a vendor that is able to host and automate much of the work the sales team had to do to answer prospect questions. While the new solution will cost $275,000 a year, it makes up that value by delaying additional hires for the sales organization and removes the workload from existing sales teams to remain laser-focused on closing deals.

Six months after implementing this third-party risk management solution the sales team's morale has increased as noted in their latest employee survey and they've reduced deal cycle times by eight days on average. They've also received positive feedback from several customers, who have appreciated how easy 100X made it to answer their cybersecurity questions and make a risk assessment of 100X's maturity.

SUMMARY

The fastest way to show your documented cybersecurity program, without going through an audit and certification that requires time, money, and resources, is to complete one of many cybersecurity questionnaires. These cover a plethora of information and can give a very granular view into your maturity when taking into account the phase your start-up is in.

Be prepared for questions or requests for more documentation, as some customers in highly regulated industries may need more than this. The total cost of acquisition (TCA) should be closely monitored as you don't want to expend $10,000 in effort to acquire a $40,000 customer.

Adding a security page to your website is a great start to publicly share that your start-up believes cybersecurity and privacy is important. Creating a cybersecurity packet will enable you to address specific customer questions when they come up in the procurement process.

ACTION PLAN

- Complete at least one vendor questionnaire that can be shared with customers.
- Create a slide in your sales deck that speaks to cybersecurity at a high level.
- Add a security section to your website that talks to your cybersecurity program at a high level.
- Take items from this chapter and go back to Chapter 2 and add these to the roadmap document you've created.

 NOTES

1. Lighthouse customers steer new customers to your start-up. These are typically early adopters that believe strongly in your product and want to help you build it. These might be great logos, such as a Fortune 100 company, or highly connected ones that are willing to sing your praises to anyone they meet.
2. https://www.sharedassessments.org
3. https://cloudsecurityalliance.org
4. https://vendorsecurityalliance.org

CHAPTER TWELVE

When the Breach Happens

There are only two types of companies – those that know they've been compromised and those that don't know.

– Dmitri Alperovitch

D ATA BREACHES ARE A FACT of life and regardless of size, all organizations are now a target. Data breaches come in many shapes and sizes. We won't specifically define a breach in this book because the term should actually be defined in your terms and conditions. There are many nuances to the terms breach, incident, event, and the like. For clarity, and to avoid pretending to be a lawyer, we'll define a breach as the unauthorized release of proprietary company information to the public Internet.

It doesn't matter if it was an employee or outside attacker, as we said it was unauthorized. It also doesn't matter what information, since we've said it was proprietary.

Looking at statistics you will most likely be affected by a breach at some point in your start-up's life cycle.[1] The odds increase as you move toward and then past the growth phase. The best way to prepare for and be antifragile is to take very specific and measured steps. Everything we have discussed up to this point will help to make your start-up capable of withstanding the impact of a breach, but there are additional measures to take.

CYBER INSURANCE

Cyber insurance is possibly the single easiest risk transference control you can put in place for your start-up. Nearly every major insurance carrier offers this type of insurance, and if you've selected a great broker they should help you navigate this sometimes convoluted world. I highly recommend using a broker, as they've had the experience of working with many insurance carriers and knowing how their customers have been supported in times of crisis. You don't want to be the first to find out your insurance provider has never dealt with a cyber insurance claim.

If you already have cyber insurance, you should meet with your broker and review your coverage. You and your founders should understand several things:

- What specifically is covered?
- What is not covered?
- Who is on your insurance carriers' panel?
- Who are the appropriate points of contact?
- What are the steps to report a breach?

Knowing what is and is not covered is important. A data breach can happen many different ways and you want to be aware of incidents that may not be covered. Some carriers also set different limits for different types of incidents. For example, an insurance carrier may set different coverage for ransomware versus a data breach caused by phishing. Your insurance broker should be able to clearly explain this to you.

Each insurance carrier will have a group of cybersecurity incident response firms that make up their panel. These are specialty firms that the insurance carrier has pre-negotiated hourly rates and other costs with.

These types of firms can charge upward of $500 per hour or more. Your insurance carrier may have negotiated better rates if you use one of those firms in the event of a data breach. This does not prevent you from setting up a retainer with other firms. There may be times where an incident has occurred and is not a data breach and you don't intend to file a claim with your carrier. You can still use a firm of your choosing to handle these events.

Finally, knowing who to contact and when is critical to make sure you get the necessary and timely support you need in a crisis. Once you have decided the need to contact your insurance broker, as an executive team there are specific steps you must take. Most brokers will want you to call them first before reaching out to the insurance carrier. They may even facilitate that contact, making sure you know the procedures as well as phone numbers, emails, and other contact methods. Depending on your industry, insurance broker, and insurance carrier, they may even have special or secure means of communication that you should set up far in advance of an event. These are all answers your insurance broker should be able to provide.

INCIDENT RESPONSE RETAINERS

You will want to put in place at least one incident response retainer with a well-established firm. This does not have to be a firm that is on your cyber insurance company's panel of incident response vendors, although it certainly can be if you want. Not every cybersecurity event will be a data breach or require you to contact your insurance broker or carrier and outside general counsel.

Having an incident response retainer in place allows you to bring in experts to investigate something that may end up being nothing; when possible these retainers should also flow through general counsel, so they are protected under privilege. Often when this happens, time is of the essence. This is not the time you want to spend negotiating terms and conditions and hourly bill rates for people, processing and transfer of data, and all the other costs these vendors charge for. Spend the time and effort to get this in place now and avoid having zero leverage when you are in a time of need. It's hard to negotiate the price of a life jacket when the boat is sinking.

You and your general counsel should pay close attention to the terms and conditions for these retainers, as we discussed in Chapter 9.

THE INCIDENT

Your insurance broker should have educated you on what to do when you have a cybersecurity incident. If they haven't, you should call them immediately and have them walk you through the steps. If they can't walk you through the steps, you should find a new broker. Understanding what steps to take during an incident is critical for both insurance claim reimbursement but also legal liabilities.

Typically, your first step will be to call your broker. They should have educated you as to the companies your insurance company has on their panel. The panel comprises the incident response firms that the insurance company has established relationships with, and negotiated rates on behalf of, all of their customers.

Next, you should determine if the incident should be under privilege. This means using an outside law firm, not your internal general counsel, to retain the incident response services from a vendor on your insurance company's panel. This is a legal danger zone and one you must take guidance from counsel on. The answer to whether to do this through privilege or not will vary greatly based on the country your business is in, the industry you operate in, and a number of other factors. If it isn't clear, seek advice from general counsel.

There will be many things in process during this event. As you determine the scope and extend of the breach you want to gather as much data as possible. Having a communications plan will be critical to set the narrative of the public perception of your handling of the incident. You don't control how you will be notified, so having templates to work from for several different audiences is key here:

- Customers
- Partners
- Investors
- Employees
- Press

These are just some of the types of individuals that will want to hear about what has happened. Messaging too soon or too late can have long-lasting negative impacts. Working closely with your communications team or external public relations (PR) firm – preferably before the event occurs – will make this a smooth process.

Be prepared for very difficult decisions. Think of worse-case scenarios for your start-up. A data breach has occurred: to stop the leak of data you need to shut off your entire cloud environment to the world. This means cutting access to all of your customers, maybe for an undetermined amount of time at that moment. We discuss these exercises next.

TABLETOP EXERCISES

I am a huge proponent of "practice makes perfect" when it comes to preparing for black swan scenarios. Tabletop exercises bring together the most critical parts of the business and work through one or more possible events. These are not unique to cybersecurity and can be applied to all parts of a business.

When carrying out a cybersecurity tabletop exercise, it is best to use a firm familiar with executing these if you have never led one yourself. This is something you would typically execute in the growth phase or beyond. These events should be built of a scope.

- What industry is your business in?
- Who are your customers?
- Where does your business operate geographically, including office locations and customer locations?
- What data do you have?

These data points will allow your firm or a third-party firm to build most likely scenarios as well as black swans and enable you and your team to work through problems in a safe and controlled way. Removing stress from a crisis to think through problems with a clear mind will allow your executive team to know exactly what risks to take, accept, transfer, mitigate, and manage.

SUMMARY

A data breach is a learning event that will ultimately make your start-up more antifragile. Data breaches are a way of life, but you can take steps right now to reduce their impact. Insurance is the greatest backstop your start-up will put in place. Having a plan will only get you so far, which is why cybersecurity is always described like the layers of an onion. There's no single action you can take that solves it all. It is many actions in concert that create a secure start-up.

Establishing relationships with vendors you can depend on during a crisis will save you sleepless nights and lower your cortisol level. Just knowing there is a fire department down the street and you have a fire extinguisher in your home can provide great ease of mind. Eventually, practicing those fire drills will make sure that when the event does happen, you are as prepared as possible. This way things are muscle memory and you are able to spend the small amount of attention you will have available dealing with unplanned things that always come up in these events.

 ACTION PLAN

- If you don't have an insurance broker, establish a relationship with one.
- Have your insurance broker talk through cyber insurance options for your start-up.
- Identify who is on the panel for the insurance company your broker helps you select.
- Review the incident response vendors on your insurance company's panel and choose at least one and no more than three to establish an MSA with.
- Once in the growth phase, execute a cybersecurity tabletop exercise.
- Add action items from this chapter to your roadmap you started developing in Chapter 2.

 NOTE

1. https://www.informationisbeautiful.net/visualizations/worlds-biggest-data-breaches-hacks/; https://haveibeenpwned.com/

CHAPTER THIRTEEN

Secure Development

You simply cannot test your application secure.

– John Steven

B UILDING A PRODUCT, whether it is software-as-a-service (SaaS), Internet of Things (IoT), smart devices, or a mobile app, must include security from the start. Doing so will allow your organization to grow and scale security with your product and keep teams focused on their primary goals. Implementing security after the fact will create unnecessary friction and delays in projects that are core to your business.

Building a minimally viable product (MVP) should have some basics of security baked into it. For example, if you are building a business intelligence SaaS product, it should, by default, communicate over HTTPS, the secure protocol used in web browsers. Consideration should be taken on how you store customer data and who has access to it. When it's just you and your fellow founders, all employees might have access to all customer data. This, however, is not appropriate when you are at 10, 50, or 1000 employees.

Secure coding is not always a straightforward process but many modern tools of today help to enable developers to avoid common mistakes. It should be noted that these automated tools can only do so much.

There are also thousands of open source and commercially available libraries of code to accelerate your development and avoid having to rebuild the wheel. Things like communication and storage encryption are something you should always use a common library for and not build in-house. There are risks that do come with using open source and commercial libraries. While vulnerabilities can exist in this code, you must also have a clear understanding of the license that goes along with it. Violating a license can be a significant financial risk to a product and business.

 ## FRAMEWORKS

We reviewed many different standards and frameworks in Chapter 10. When it comes to developing software there is no shortage of frameworks to do so. While there are many development-focused frameworks like old-school Waterfall or new-school Agile, we won't review those here. There are many books on those topics already. There are now security-specific standards and maturity models just for developing secure code.

BSIMM

The Building Security in Maturity Model[1] (BSIMM) is a model created by Synopsys (formerly Cigital). The model includes 121 activates in four domains:

Governance
Intelligence
SSDL touchpoints
Deployment

Like other frameworks and models in this chapter, BSIMM is something to be aware of during the formation and validation phase and something to strongly consider in growth phase. There is also nothing stopping you from using the model in the formation phase as you create your software

Governance	Intelligence	SSDL Touchpoints	Deployment
Strategy and Metrics	Attack Models	Architecture Analysis	Penetration Testing
Compliance and Policy	Security Features and Design	Code Review	Software Environment
Training	Standards and Requirements	Security Testing	Configuration Management and Vulnerability Management

FIGURE 13.1 The Four Pillars of BSIMM and High-Level Components
Source: https://www.reshiftsecurity.com/developer-first-security-shifting-security-left-with-a-plan/

development life cycle. While it is not a how-to-guide, you can use frameworks and models as a guide to form good habits in your development. Figure 13.1 shows the four pillars of BSIMM and what is typically included in those pillars.

OpenSAMM

The Software Assurance Maturity Model (SAMM)[2] is an open framework developed by OWASP, which was discussed in Chapter 10. OpenSAMM is a framework start-ups can use to bake in cybersecurity competence in their SDLC as well as measure the maturity. It is free to use and is widely contributed to in the cybersecurity and software development communities. Figure 13.2 shows the OpenSAMM framework pillars and practices included in each.

CMMI

The Capability Maturity Model Integration (CMMI) is a long-standing model for software development maturity.[3] It was developed by Carnegie Mellon University and the first version was released in 2002. This replaced its predecessor capability maturity model (CMM), which was created in and maintained since 1987. CMMI is notable as it is typically a requirement on US government software development contracts. Figure 13.3 shows

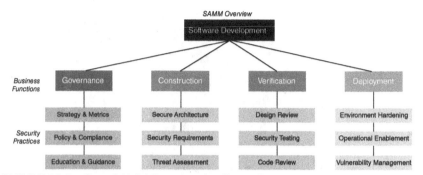

FIGURE 13.2 OpenSAMM Framework Pillar and Practices
Source: https://www.reshiftsecurity.com/developer-first-security-shifting-security-left-with-a-plan/

Figure 7—CMMI Maturity Levels

MATURITY LEVEL 5	Optimizing	**Stable and flexible:** Organization is focused on continuous improvement and is built to pivot and respond to opportunity and change. The organization's stability provides a platform for agility and innovation.	5
MATURITY LEVEL 4	Quantitatively Managed	**Measured and controlled:** Organization is data-driven with quantitative performance improvement objectives that are predictable and align to meet the needs of internal and external stakeholders.	4
MATURITY LEVEL 3	Defined	**Proactive, rather than reactive:** Organization-wide standards provide guidance across projects, programs, and portfolios.	3
MATURITY LEVEL 2	Managed	**Managed on the project level:** Projects are planned, performed, measured, and controlled.	2
MATURITY LEVEL 1	Initial	**Unpredictable and reactive:** Work gets completed, but is often delayed and over budget.	1

Source: CMMI Institute, Rerinted with permission.

FIGURE 13.3 CMMI Maturity Levels
Source: https://www.isaca.org/resources/isaca-journal/issues/2017/volume-4/enterprise-security-architecturea-top-down-approach

the five maturity levels and descriptions of CMMI. The five levels to the maturity model are:

Level 1 – Initial
Level 2 – Managed

Level 3 – Defined
Level 4 – Quantitatively Managed
Level 5 – Optimizing

 ## MICROSOFT SDL

Microsoft Security Development LifeCycle (SDL)[4] is a secure development process Microsoft created in 2004 and shared publicly in 2008 for others to adopt. The goal of the framework is to reduce and eliminate security risks from code that is developed. There are seven phases in the Microsoft SDL, each with several processes and practices that should be implemented. Figure 13.4 shows the Microsoft SDL workflow.

 ## PRE-COMMIT

When you are developing your code, you will most likely be doing this on your laptop. Maybe you already have a very advanced setup and are using a remote development environment for higher security, like AWS Workspaces. But for this chapter we will assume it's on your laptop. From here we will also assume you've already implemented the important controls discussed in Chapters 3 through 5.

When you are developing code in your Integrated Development Environment (IDE) there are now many useful tools that add on to almost all the popular IDEs available today that act as spell-checkers for secure code. Many free options check for basics like OWASP Top 10 that we reviewed

Training	Requirements	Design	Imlementation	Verification	Release	Response
	Establish Security Requirements	Establish Design Requirements	Use Approved Tools	Dynamic Analysis	Incident Response Plan	
Core Security Training	Create Quality Gates / Bug Bars	Analyze Attack Surface	Deprecate Unsafe Functions	Fuzz Testing	Final Security Review	Execute Incident Response Plan
	Security & Privacy Risk Assessment	Threat Modeling	Static Analysis	Attack Surface Review	Release Archive	

FIGURE 13.4 Microsoft SDL Workflow
Source: https://social.technet.microsoft.com/wiki/contents/articles/7100.the-security-development-lifecycle.aspx

in Chapter 10. These tools won't catch every single possible security issue, but they are great at capturing low hanging fruit,[5] which many times is the main cause of a data breach. Focus on the basics and save the advanced solutions that only improve your start-up by 1% for after the growth phase.

 ## INTEGRATED DEVELOPMENT ENVIRONMENT

As a founder, you are most likely the CEO, janitor, site reliability engineer (SRE), and developer. We've discussed keeping your devices secure as a first step. The next most important place to bake security into your product is right where your product starts to come to life, your Integrated Development Environment, or IDE. Here you will write the code that becomes the next unicorn product. There are numerous IDEs and we can't possibly cover each here. Some of the most popular ones include Microsoft Visual Studio, NetBeans, PyCharm, IntelliJ IDEA, Eclipse, and Xcode, to name a few.

Many of these IDEs either include security checks or have supported add-ons that build in additional functionality to help check code for security flaws as you write. There are many variables to these tools that will require additional research on your part, depending on the IDE and language you are developing in.

 ## COMMIT

You will also most likely be using a cloud repository for your code like GitHub, or maybe you have one hosted internally in your cloud environment, like GitLab. Either way there are more tools that can be applied here to scan and check code for issues that may not have been caught and corrected in the pre-commit phase.

Once code is checked into your code repository you have another chance to scan that code for vulnerabilities and flaws. This is typically referred to as static code analysis (SCA). There are free open source and paid commercial tools that support many of the most common code repositories and development languages.

Open source libraries deserve a special call out in this section due to the highly common dependencies built on open source code. While using open source can accelerate your development, it still introduces risks, sometimes more so, than writing the code yourself. While using open source can introduce software vulnerabilities, you now must address the legal requirements of the specific license in which the open source software is available. Your general counsel can certainly help navigate these licenses; like many start-ups you will most likely have tens or hundreds of open source components in your product. At that scale you will most likely need a software solution to manage these.

BUILD

The further we travel down the continuous development/continuous integration (CD/CI) pipeline, the options grow exponentially for baking in cybersecurity. Entire books are devoted just to this single topic in this chapter alone. Typical security testing of software that is compiled or "built" can include dynamic code analysis (DCA), web application scanning, and penetration testing. Because the functionality of software can differ so greatly – for example, firmware for a field-programmable gate array (FPGA)-based device or a web application used in a web browser – it is best, as a start-up, to delay purchasing software but instead to identify a penetration testing vendor that specializes in the type of software you are building.

PENETRATION TESTING

Penetration testing, or pentesting, is not only helpful in improving the security of the product you are developing but also a requirement for several of the compliance, regulatory, and certification standards we discussed in Chapter 9 and Chapter 10. Penetration testing is the act of attempting to discover and exploit vulnerabilities in a system.

This is typically always a service provided by many firms; however, there are some attempting to develop software to automate this type of work. This automated penetration testing or pentest-as-a-service (PaaS), not to be confused with platform-as-a-service (PaaS), is still relatively new as at the time of writing, and the efficacy is not yet established.

The benefits from paying for a penetration test of your product, whether it is a piece of hardware, mobile, web app, or system-on-a-chip (SoaC) is highly dependent on who is actually conducting the penetration test. The type of penetration test as well as applicable scoping will affect the price. This could range from $10,000 for, say, a very simple web app or API to well over $100,000. Some firms you can start your search with include:

Praetorian
Bishop Fox
Soteria
TrustedSec
Black Hills Information Security

 ## SUMMARY

When you are baking cybersecurity into your start-up, you must also be baking it into the product you are developing. The cybersecurity onion layers must be applied everywhere in order to create a resilient system that will scale. Deploying insecure code into a secure Docker container introduces risks and vulnerabilities regardless of how well you've secured the container.

 ## ACTION PLAN

- Install an IDE add-on to scan your code as you write for security issues for the specific language you are using. If you are using something obscure you may have trouble finding a free solution.
- Integrate a static or dynamic code analysis tool with your code repository, as well as build server.
- Have a plan of what to do when you find bugs. You don't want to wait until you are about to push to production to find an issue. The easier you can make the discovery and correction the more time you will save.
- Take action items from this chapter and add them to your roadmap you've been building from Chapter 2.

NOTES

1. https://www.bsimm.com/
2. https://www.opensamm.org/
3. https://cmmiinstitute.com/
4. https://social.technet.microsoft.com/wiki/contents/articles/7100.the-security-development-lifecycle.aspx
5. Low hanging fruit usually refers to quick and easy wins. Problems that are easy and cheap to solve.

CHAPTER FOURTEEN

Third-Party Risk

Yeah, risk is good.

– Dade Murphy, *Hackers*

D ATA BREACHES VIA VENDORS and third parties is a significant risk to businesses, even start-ups. The convenience and reliability of software-as-a-service (SaaS) products to run your business is appealing and valuable. You must be aware of what data and, in some cases, what access to your data and systems you give to third parties. You may even be working with a start-up just like yours reading this same book.

Outside counsel should always be consulted before signing any terms and conditions, to make sure the third party is implementing the appropriate level of protection around your data or access to your data; and also to make sure you fully understand what data you will be giving that vendor. Requirements like General Data Protection Regulation (GDPR) require you maintain a data map of your vendors and what data they have when it comes to personally identifiable information (PII). However, your company should be concerned about both PII and your proprietary data.

While there are companies that can help assess the risk of a third-party vendor or build GDPR-compliant data maps, even a simple spreadsheet is enough to get you started. Keeping a list of your vendors and the data they have will go a long way as you scale and expand your start-up.

TERMS AND CONDITIONS

Just like we reviewed terms from customers in Chapter 9, you must also review the terms and conditions of your vendors to ensure they are following proper due diligence when protecting your data and your customers' data. Your ability to influence these terms in a substantial way will be affected by the size of the vendor and your spend with them. This is where the risk–reward trade-off comes in. If you are only paying $10 per month for a service, it is unlikely that they would accept any changes to their terms. This is where legal counsel can provide great value to make sure you are not taking on unnecessary risks, and that the reward of using that service outweighs those risks.

You may have already come across mature procurement processes with your own customers, so you may know what they look for when reviewing a new vendor. It is not of great value to develop a mature process like a larger business, so you should ask two questions before conducting any type of cybersecurity review of a vendor.

Will the vendor process, access, store, or transmit sensitive data?
Will the vendor access systems or services that process, access, store, or transmit sensitive data?

Another important consideration to be aware of is the jurisdiction of the vendor and where their services are hosted. This is especially important to be compliant with regulations like GDPR. Depending on what type of data your business processes, you'll need to make sure, for example, that EU citizen data remains in the EU as defined by GDPR in most cases.

SHOULD I REVIEW THIS VENDOR?

Will the vendor process, access, store, or transmit sensitive data? You must first define what sensitive data is for your organization. An easy example would be credit card data. If the answer to the question is yes, you should review the vendor more thoroughly. Sensitive data may also be a proprietary AI or ML algorithm, or non-volatile battery compound, or designs for a more energy-efficient windshield. Whatever it is, you must first define that for your organization.

Will the vendor access systems or services that process, access, store, or transmit sensitive data? A good example would be a vendor that could add more value to an existing solution, such as sales insights to your deal process (e.g., a vendor that would access your customer relationship management [CRM] system and provide better deal metrics to increase deal size and velocity). Or maybe it is a vendor that will help control cloud costs and needs access to your authentication system to detect users logging into SaaS.

WHAT TO ASK AND LOOK FOR

At the most basic level, does the vendor have a cybersecurity program? You'll want to look for all the basic components we've discussed in this book. To speed up your review and make it as painless as possible for both you and the vendor, here are some questions to ask.

- Do you have certifications or audits that can be provided, like ISO 27001, SOC2, PCI DSS, HITRUST, NIST?
- Do you have questionnaires that you can share, such as SIG, CAIQ, VSA?
- Can you provide the latest penetration test of the solution we are buying?
- What endpoint detection and response (EDR) do you use?
- How is the environment monitored 24x7x365 for threats?
- Who does the vendor have an incident response retainer with?
- What is the total cybersecurity insurance coverage?
- At an executive level, who is responsible for cybersecurity and privacy?

You should expect to be asked to execute a non-disclosure agreement (NDA) to get answers to most of these and other questions. While you should make a note that you did review their security, unless precluded by laws, regulations, or contractual requirements, try to avoid keeping the data. Things like penetration test reports, audit reports, and the like are sensitive documents that contain material information. You don't want to be responsible for their safe keeping.

So what answers should you expect? As they say, well, it depends. Let's look at extreme examples. Take, for instance, a vendor that is going to process and store DNA information. You will want explicit answers for every question, in verbose detail. Or, on the other side of the risk scale, this vendor will process the geo coordinates of funny videos uploaded with their viral app.

This is more nuanced and not as obvious. If all the vendor does is strip metadata from a video file but does not process or save the content, less clear answers to these questions might not be a big deal. Or maybe they will process the geo coordinates and associate that with the user for targeted advertisements. In that case you'd want to see more clear maturity of their security controls.

If you have some type of internal ticketing system like JIRA, you could use that to create a ticket and make note of the information received, any issues discovered, and what documents you reviewed.

There are also many vendors that claim to make this process easier for you and your vendors, all while reducing cyber risk for you. After being on both ends of the vendor review process I can confirm this is simply not true. These firms simply inject more cost into the procurement process, for both the vendor and customer, all while single handedly driving a wedge between the business and cybersecurity.

There are several open source tools you can use to quickly assess the maturity of an organization's cybersecurity program.

Verify DMARC Settings

Domain-based message authentication, reporting, and conformance (DMARC)[1] is a control that vendors can put in place to prevent their domain name from being spoofed in emails. There are many tools available to do this and you can find them with a simple Google search, such as "verify dmarc." You will want to look for indications as to whether this setting is enabled in their domain name server (DNS) email settings. The vendor should have DMARC setup and configured for 100% reject.

If it is not enabled or is set to reject 0%, this shows their program may not be very mature. DMARC protects the sending domain from attackers spoofing emails from that exact domain. This is a relatively easy setting for organizations to make. It is even easier if there is only one sending domain that they must protect.

If it is not enabled, this shouldn't make you run for the hills, but ask more questions as to why it is not enabled, and how they are protecting email spoofing from their domain.

Check TLS Certificates

Transport Layer Security (TLS) certificates are what underpin the security of browsing the Internet. It put the "S" in HTTPS. A website that wants to provide a secure connection to their users will have a certificate installed and available to users. This all happens in the background automatically between your web browser, like Chrome, Firefox, Safari, or Edge, and the secure website you are visiting.

Sites like ssllabs.com will let you scan a website and receive a letter grade report back on the certificate security of that website. While the information provided is extremely verbose and technical, anything below a grade B, meaning C through F, is a warning sign. You might see sites that support supposed vulnerable and deprecated versions of TLS; this sometimes is a requirement for them to support customers unable to upgrade for a variety of reasons. Also, most modern attacks against TLS are academic in nature and require a nation-state level of computing power to take advantage of said vulnerabilities.

Check the Security Headers of the Website

The security headers offered by a website also give you a glimpse into the maturity of their overall cybersecurity program. Sites like securityheaders .com allow you to put in a domain and receive a letter grade for the security headers they have present on the website. These headers prevent a variety of attacks against that specific website and are usually trivial to implement.

A caveat here is that many vendors don't actually host their own website. If it is a SaaS application, you will want to check the URL of the

SaaS application. A typical example might be something like "app.vendor .com." Even you as the founder reading this book might not even be hosting your own website in your own cloud environment. That simply isn't "keeping the main thing the main thing." So you might host with a website-hosting provider like so many other start-ups. This is where things can get tricky, if you haven't already noticed that about cybersecurity and security features.

Many website hosting providers have various tiers that you can purchase, like any other software-as-a-service (SaaS) vendor. Unfortunately, it is typical for most vendors to keep security features behind more expensive tiers, leaving more frugal customers exposed. Don't be surprised to see low letter grades when running your vendors through this search.

You can ask about it, but if their front-door website has nothing to do with the product you are buying, then this is an overall low risk if they haven't bought the next highest tier in order to turn on these features.

 SUMMARY

Risk comes in many forms for any business. Every start-up, including yours, will most likely depend on many vendors to build and support the business. Just remember, every risk can be mitigated in some way. So just because a vendor is risky doesn't mean you should find someone else to do business with.

 ACTION PLAN

- Document your vendors just like you are documenting your assets. Keep track of who you do business with. This is pretty easy to pull from the finance system you are most likely using. But you will eventually want to make note of what vendors have critical data, or that you've reviewed their security. These reviews are requirements for certifications like SOC2.

- Keep a checklist of what you will look at with each vendor and remember to consider their size. A start-up in the formation phase will be less mature than a 100-year-old institution.
- Take any action items from this chapter and add them to the roadmap you've been building from Chapter 2.

NOTE

1. https://dmarc.org/

CHAPTER FIFTEEN

Bringing It All Together

Make it work.

– Tim Gunn, *Project Runway*

W E HAVE COVERED A LOT IN THIS BOOK, and while it might not all have stuck, I hope you will use this book as a reference in your journey to a unicorn exit. The topic of cybersecurity can be complex, overwhelming, and even sometimes insulting. I hope this book has broken down barriers for you and either given you that "ah-ha" moment or armed you with the information to ask better informed questions of your fellow founders, investors, customers, and vendors.

Cybersecurity doesn't have to be a mysterious magician in the background preventing doom at every moment of the day. It should be valued and prioritized like all the other needs of your start-up. You will most likely use accounting software early on to keep track of spending, since you will eventually have to file taxes. You don't need to be a CPA to do that and you don't need to be a 10x CISO to build your cybersecurity program.

I started this book by asking you to keep in mind the quote from *7 Habits of Highly Effective People* where Stephen Covey states, "The main thing is to keep the main thing the main thing." This is a reminder – after going through the topics in this book, each of which has numerous books dedicated to it – to keep it simple. When you are building an MVP you should be building the equivalent cybersecurity program to match your product's needs, your customers' needs, and your start-up's needs.

This book has been amazing to write and I hope it brings value to your team and start-up. I hope I have both answered questions and given you new questions to ask. Most importantly, I hope you feel informed enough to start on your journey to baking cybersecurity into your company, from founding to exit.

For more content please visit www.startupsecure.io

To recap what you should do next:

- Determine what stage your business is at: formation, validation, or growth.
- Define and write down who your ideal customers are.
- Write down what industries they are in.
- Write down what data, if any, you will process, store, access, or in any way have access to.
- Go create a strong passphrase and set it on your laptop.
- Purchase a physical multi-factor authentication token.
- Sign up for a password manager:
  - Set a strong passphrase, different than any others you are using
  - Set up hardware-based multi-factor authentication
  - Get all of your accounts loaded in it.
- Set up a soft, multi-factor authentication token app on your phone.
- Set your most critical accounts to the highest possible security settings and enable multi-factor authentication on all of them.
- Determine what operating systems you need to support to install endpoint detection and response (EDR) or endpoint protection (EPP).
  - Determine if you need the solution managed; this will depend on if you are in the formation, validation, or growth stage.
  - Review terms and conditions with your general counsel.
  - Be cautious locking into long-term contracts if you have not used the vendor before. If cost is the reason to purchase a 3-year term, then make sure you have strong termination rights.
  - Deploy the solution as soon as possible.

- Make sure your home wireless router has strong authentication setup, a passphrase you store in your password manager. If it is controlled through a cloud app, turn on multi-factor authentication if that is an option.
- Before you move into a co-working space or use a public wireless network, make sure your device is secure, as we discussed in Chapters 3 and 4.
- Turn on all security features on your enterprise wireless network when you move into a leased space.
- Apply what you learned in Chapter 3 to your cloud account. Protect those credentials at all costs and use them only for their recommended purpose as directed by your cloud provider.
- Enable multi-factor authentication on your cloud provider account.
- If possible use the most up-to-date workload images supplied by the cloud provider. If your product needs something more bespoke, make sure you've accounted for how you will patch it when it is running in production.
- If you have already selected an endpoint detection and response solution, which we dove into in Chapter 4, and it supports your cloud workloads, deploy it as you are building the product. You want to make sure it does not interfere with what you are building. Pay attention to resource usage by the EDR and central processing unit (CPU); memory and disk space all cost money.
- If you are building a fully containerized environment make sure you are again accounting for patching. Vendors are not perfect and will always release patches. Your product should account for this.
- Documenting, as much as you can, the software-as-a-service (SaaS) tools you are already using, like Google Workspace or Microsoft Office 365, can help you stay organized to a point. A good rule of thumb is that once the data no longer fits on one screen in your spreadsheet, it might be time to buy a solution to automatically manage that data.
- Make sure you can always provide a list of all the systems you have – laptops, mobile devices, cloud workloads, containers, and even software libraries you might build into your product. Auditors will want this, and if you are in the small percentage of start-ups that must obtain a certification like SOC2 or ISO 27001 in the formation or

validation phase, you will need this information immediately. We talk about these certifications in Chapter 10.

- When it is time to hire your first cybersecurity role, define your needs for the candidate.
  - Determine if those needs are for an engineer or executive.
  - Engage with your talent acquisition partner or recruiting firm.
  - If you don't yet have a recruiting firm, begin interviewing firms that specialize in the type of candidate you are looking for. Not all firms recruit engineers or executives.
- Work with general counsel or outside legal to build legal documents such as MSAs, T&Cs, and DPAs. Including languages and sections around security is great to state your terms up front instead of letting the customer propose them.
- If you have contracts already in place, review them for any security provisions with legal and cybersecurity advisors.
- If you will do business in the EU, look for recommendations on legal firms to use that are based in the EU. They can assist with GDPR, and some will act as your DPO. GDPR requires your DPO is an EU citizen.
- Define what industries you will either operate in or sell into.
- Review the relevant regulations with general counsel to determine what you must comply with.
- Review the necessary applicable regulations to incorporate those standards into your cybersecurity roadmap and strategy.
- If you have not yet hired internal general counsel or outside counsel, now is the time to do so.
- Write down the answers to the questions in this chapter.
- Based on those answers go back to Chapters 9 and 10 and write down what you may need to comply with.
- Reference those controls against what you have already put in place from Chapters 3 through 6.
- Complete at least one vendor questionnaire that can be shared with customers.
- Create a slide in your sales deck that speaks to cybersecurity at a high level.
- If you don't have an insurance broker, establish a relationship with one.

- Have your insurance broker talk through cyber insurance options for your start-up.
- Identify who is on the panel for the insurance company your broker helps you select.
- Review the incident response vendors on your insurance company's panel and choose at least one and no more than three to establish an MSA with.
- Once in the growth phase, execute a cybersecurity tabletop exercise.
- Install an IDE add-on to scan your code as you write for security issues for the specific language you are using. If you are using something obscure, you may have trouble finding a free solution.
- Integrate a static or dynamic code analysis tool with your code repository, as well as build server.
- Have a plan of what to do when you find bugs. You don't want to wait until you are about to push to production to find an issue. The easier you can make the discovery and correction the more time you will save.
- Document your vendors just like you are documenting your assets. Keep track of who you do business with. This is pretty easy to pull from the finance system you are most likely using. But you will eventually want to make note of what vendors have critical data, or that you've reviewed their security. These reviews are requirements for certifications like SOC2.
- Keep a checklist of what you will look at with each vendor and remember to consider their size. A start-up in the formation phase will be less mature than a 100-year-old institution.

Glossary

3PAO Abbreviation for third-party assessment organization in FedRAMP.

5220.22-M United States Department of Defense insider threat standard.

Adobe Acrobat Word processor developed by Adobe.

Advanced Encryption Standard A popular encryption standard to encrypt data at rest.

AEs Acronym for account executive, a role within a sales organization.

Agile A software development methodology.

Agri-tech Agriculture technology sector.

Alibaba Cloud Infrastructure-as-a-service platform developed by Alibaba.

Amazon Web Service Infrastructure-as-a-service platform developed by Amazon.

American Institute of Certified Public Accountants United States organization that sets accounting standards.

Android A mobile operating system for phone and tablets created by Google.

Anonymization Making it so the user or source of an action is not attributable to a person or the true identity of a system.

Ansible Software to manage Linux systems.

Antivirus Software that protects computers from malicious software.

Apple Computer and mobile device manufacture.

Apple App Store Smartphone app repository to download apps for Apple devices.

Apple iCloud Cloud-based storage service sold by Apple.

Apple MacBooks Laptops developed by Apple.

Apple MacOS   Computer operating system developed by Apple.

Apps   A common term that typically refers to software that you install on your smartphone.

Authenticator   Software that provides additional security verification when determining if a user is allowed to access a system.

Authy   Multi-factor authentication service provider.

AWS Workspaces   Cloud-based desktop terminals developed by Amazon Web Services.

Azure   Infrastructure-as-a-service platform developed by Microsoft.

B2B   Abbreviation for business-to-business.

Best-effort   When an organization agrees to terms in a contract but will not guarantee specifics.

BlackBerry   Smartphone and business software manufacturer.

Bring Your Own Keys   A feature of some software-as-a-service providers that allow customers to use and control their own encryption keys.

Broker-dealers   Financial institution designation under FINRA.

Business-to-business   Organizations that sell to other businesses and not directly to consumers.

C2M2   Abbreviation for United States Department of Energy standard cybersecurity capabilities and maturity model.

California Consumer Privacy Act   A law in the State of California that dictates specific privacy rights for consumers that are citizens of that state.

Card Industry   Credit card industry.

Card-not-present   A credit card transaction, typically over the Internet, when a physical credit card is not swiped through a machine or presented physically to the merchant.

Carnegie Mellon University   A private research university in the United States.

Carve-outs   Specifics of a contract that are separated, removed, or omitted from the main contract or subsequent addendums, exhibits, etc.

Checkmarx   A software company.

Chief security officer   The most senior executive in an organization who is typically responsible for both cybersecurity and physical security.

Chrome   A web browser developed by Google.

Chrysler   Automotive manufacturer.

Cigital   Former name for Synopsys, a software services company.

Cisco   Network equipment manufacture.

CIS Critical Security Controls   A cybersecurity controls framework.

CISO   Abbreviation for chief information security officer, the most senior executive in an organization responsible for cybersecurity.

Click-through   Typically the pop-up message one receives prior to using software that requires the user to agree to specific terms by clicking a button to acknowledge that they read and agree to said terms.

Cloud Access Security Brokers   Software that enables secure remote access to resources.

CloudFormation   Infrastructure-as-code-service developed by Amazon Web Services.

Cloud Platform   Common term referring to infrastructure-as-a-service providers.

Cloud Security Alliance   An independent organization that has created a set of standards specific for cloud.

Cloud Security Alliance STAR   Framework and certification standard created by the Cloud Security Alliance.

Cloud Security Posture Management   Software for maintaining the secure configuration of infrastructure-as-a-service platforms.

CMMI Maturity Levels   Software code quality measurement standard.

Compromise   The act of maliciously gaining access to a device, system, user credential, access, or data.

Consumer Financial Protection Bureau   United States federal agency.

Critical Start   Managed detection and response vendor.

Cyber Essentials Basic   A certification level within UK Cyber Essentials.

Cyber Essentials Plus   A certification level within UK Cyber Essentials.

Cybersecurity Capabilities Maturity Model   A cybersecurity model developed and maintained by the United States Department of Energy.

Data Breach   An event in which data is accessed by an unauthorized party.

Data center   Large building containing thousands of servers.

Data Processing Agreement   A contractual document, part of GDPR and CCPA.

Data Protection Officer   An individual or organization that resides in the European Union that represents a company for GDPR.

Deidentification   The action of modifying data in such a way as to remove data or metadata that could reveal what or who that data is about or attributed to.

Deidentified   Data that has already been modified to remove data or metadata that could reveal what or who the data is about or attributed to.

Deprovisioned   The state of a user's identity after termination when all access is suspended.

Deprovisioning   The process of removing all of a user's access after termination.

Device Management   The business process of acquiring, maintaining, and deprovisioning a technology device.

DevOps   Abbreviation of development operations, a business function that supports the creation of software.

Discover Financial Services   A large credit card issuer.

Docker   Software container technology.

DPA   Abbreviation for data processing agreement.

Drive   Cloud-based file storage service from Google.

Dropbox   A popular cloud-based file storage service.

EDR   Abbreviation of endpoint detection and response, software that protects systems from malicious software and actions.

Emails   Electronic mail, a form of sending messages over the Internet.

Email Security Gateway   Software that adds security to email systems to defend against things such as phishing.

End of Life   When software is no longer supported or updated by the manufacturer.

Endpoint Detection and Response   Software that protects systems from malicious software and user actions, replacing antivirus.

Entitlements   Attributes assigned to users or systems that determine access to systems or data.

Epp   Abbreviation of endpoint protection platform, software that protects systems from malicious software and actions.

ES-C2M2   An additional standard within the cybersecurity capabilities and maturity model.

Ethernet   A network protocol.

European Court of Justice   The governing body for GDPR.

Excel   Spreadsheet software developed by Microsoft.

Exploit   Software or an action that takes advantage of a vulnerability in a system.

Fast ID Online   Authentication standard.

Federal Deposit Insurance Corporation   A United States federal agency.

Federal Energy Regulatory Commission in the United States   A United States federal agency.

Federal Reserve Board of Governors   A body of organizations that sets regulations for the Federal Reserve.

FedRAMP   A United States federal government standard and certification.

Fintech   Abbreviation of financial technology, a specific sector of businesses.

Firefox   A popular web browser developed by the Mozilla Foundation.

Friedman, Milton   A well-known author and economist.

Fyde Barracuda CloudGen   CASB vendor.

Gartner   Independent body that reviews software.

Gartner Magic Quadrant   A scoring and ranking methodology developed by Gartner.

General Data Protection Regulation   A law in the European Union that dictates specifics for privacy rights of consumers that are citizens in the European Union.

GitHub   A cloud-based software repository for storing and managing software source code.

GitLab   A software repository developer.

Gmail   An email service developed by Google.

Google   An American multinational technology company specializing in Internet-related services and products.

Google Authenticator   Multi-factor authentication app used on smartphones.

Google Cloud Platform   Infrastructure-as-a-service platform developed by Google.

Google Docs   Cloud-based word processor developed by Google.

Google Play   Software repository for Android devices.

Google Titan   Physical security tokens for authentication developed by Google.

Google Workspace   Business software suite developed by Google.

Google Workspace for Business   A tier of service offered by Google Workspace.

Greenfield   New and mostly unbuild environment.

G Suite   Cloud-based business applications developed by Google.

Hardcode   The act of putting sensitive or secret data directly into software code.

Hardcoded   A common phrase to describe when information is written directly into software code instead of being referenced as a variable, such as saving a password in your software source code.

Helpdesk   A function of IT that provides direct support to end users and troubleshooting.

Hitch Partners   Recruiting firm specializing in CISO/CSO searches and placements.

HITECH Act   United States federal law for health data.

Https   The protocol that enables secure web browsing.

Human-developed   Software that is not created by automated means with artificial intelligence or machine learning software.

IaaS   Abbreviation for infrastructure-as-a-service.

IASME Consortium   An organization in the United Kingdom that governs UK Cyber Essentials certification.

iCloud   Cloud-based storage service sold by Apple.

IDE   Acronym for integrated developer environment.

Industry-specific   Specifics in the contract that are only related to that type of business.

Information Security Management System   A specific designation of a cybersecurity program within ISO 27001 standard.

Initial Public Offering   When a private company is listed on a public stock exchange, allowing the general public to purchase shares in that company.

Integrated Development Environment   Software in which a developer writes software code.

Internet   An interconnected global network.

Internet of Things   Devices other than traditional computers or phones that are connected to the Internet.

Internet Service Providers   Companies that provide internet access directly to businesses and consumers.

iOS   Smartphone operating system developed by Apple

IoT   Abbreviation of Internet of Things.

iPhone   Smartphone hardware developed by Apple.

ISA-62443   An international standard.

Joint Authorization Board   An organizational body within FedRAMP.

Keychain   Software built into MacOS for storing secrets.

KPIs   Abbreviation for key performance indicators, a business metric to measure and monitor business systems or processes.

Kubernetes   Software for managing containers in cloud environments.

LastPass   Password manager developed by LogMeIn.

Lee Iacocca   Former CEO of Chrysler.

Linux   Common operating system in cloud environments and SaaS vendors.

Mac   Common term to refer to both computers developed by Apple as well as the MacOS operating system.

MacOS   Computer operating system developed by Apple.

MasterCard   A multinational financial services corporation.

MDM   Abbreviation for mobile device management, software used to maintain user endpoints.

MDR   Abbreviation of managed detection and response, a vendor category of companies that provide services to manage all or parts of your cybersecurity tools.

Microsoft   An American multinational technology company.

Microsoft Active Directory   Directory software used to manage users and systems, developed by Microsoft.

Microsoft Azure   Infrastructure-as-a-service offering from Microsoft.

Microsoft Defender   Endpoint detection and response software developed by Microsoft.

Microsoft Office   Business software suite developed by Microsoft.

Microsoft OneDrive   Cloud-based file storage developed by Microsoft.

Microsoft SDL   A software development standard created by Microsoft.

Microsoft Teams   Cloud-based chat platform developed by Microsoft.

Microsoft Visual Studio   An IDE developed by Microsoft.

Microsoft Word   Word processor software developed by Microsoft.

Minimally Viable Product   The point at which a product has met a threshold to be useable by general customers.

Misconfigurations   System settings that when set cause unintended system problems or create vulnerabilities.

Mobile Device Management   Software used to maintain end user systems.

National Credit Union Administration   United States federal agency that governs credit unions.

National Institute of Standard Technology   United States non-regulatory federal agency.

New York Department of Financial Services Cybersecurity Regulation   Regulation in the State of New York that requires specific controls for financial institutions.

NIST Cybersecurity Framework   A document of controls and tools developed by NIST.

NIST HIPAA Security Toolkit Application   A set of documents for health data cybersecurity.

Non-conformities   Negative findings from an auditing showing non-compliance with a standard.

Non-disclosure   An agreement between two or more parties that defines confidentiality for specific information shared between said parties.

North American Electric Reliability Corporation   Government agency responsible for regulating electricity in North America.

OAuth   Authentication standard.

Offboarding   The process of removing a user from an organization.

Office 365   Business productivity software suite developed by Microsoft.

Office for Civil Rights   An office within the United States Health and Human services responsible for governing health data.

OKRs   Abbreviation of objectives and key results, a methodology for measuring and monitoring business processes and systems.

Onboarded The process of activating a customer on your product or platform in order to accelerate time to value for that customer.

Onboarding The process of providing new employees with required tools and access to perform job functions.

ONG-C2M2 A subset of the cybersecurity capabilities and maturity model.

Open Source Software that is free to use under various licenses.

OpenID Authentication standard.

OpenSAMM A software development quality and security framework.

Operating System The underlying software that is used on computers and smartphones.

Outlook Email client that is used on desktop and smartphones developed by Microsoft.

Outsource The act of engaging a third party to conduct specific tasks or procedures on behalf of the business.

Outsourcing The act of engaging a vendor to perform business function and processes on behalf of the company.

OWASP Top 10 The top programmatic flaws as described by OWASP.

Passcode Typically all-numeric password used to secure smartphones.

Passphrase A long, hard-to-guess sentence or phrase used as a password.

Payment Card Industry Data Security Standard A standard that governs credit card data security.

PCI Security Standards Council An independent organization that sets cybersecurity standards for credit card data.

Pentest The act of testing software for exploitable vulnerabilities.

Pentest-as-a-service Continuous penetration testing provided by a vendor.

Pentesting The act of testing software for exploitable vulnerabilities.

Phishing A malicious email that attempts to get the recipient to take some action.

Platform-as-a-service A software provider that sells and manages the middle layer of technology between infrastructure and an application.

Ponemon Institute Independent cybersecurity research organization.

PowerPoint Business presentation software developed by Microsoft.

Pre-Commit Before code is pushed into the main repository.

Pre-IPO   The stage of a company prior to becoming publicly listed on a stock exchange.

Privacy Shield   A previous standard for privacy rights of EU citizen data sharing between the United States and EU.

Prosumer   Software or hardware that is marketed to users with more advanced features than consumer products but not as much as enterprise products.

Puppet   System management software.

QR code   A two-demensional graphical representation of some data that can be scanned with a smartphone or other device.

Ransomware   Malicious software that encrypts user data and demands payment to release the data.

SaaS   Abbreviation for software-as-a-service.

Safari   A web browser developed by Apple.

Saltstack   System management software.

Sarbanes–Oxley Act   United States law governing publicly traded companies.

Schrems II   A court case that invalidated Privacy Shield.

Screenshot   The act of taking a picture of a computer or smartphone screen, typically with built-in functionality of that device.

Secure Access Service Edge   Software for secure remote access to resources.

Secure Shell   A text-based remote access tool used to administer systems.

Security Incident Event Management   Software that correlates security events from many sources and creates new alerts.

Self-assessment   When an organization conducts a review of some standard on itself without an independent third party.

Series A   A capital funding event start-ups execute typically after an initial seed funding round to raise capital to build their product.

Service Agreements   Contractual documents stipulating the type of services a customer is buying.

Shared Assessments   An independent organization that has developed security and privacy questionnaires to evaluate vendors.

Side Channel Security   Cybersecurity vendor.

SIG Full   Questionnaire developed by Shared Assessments for cybersecurity and privacy.

SIG Lite   A subset of questions from SIG Full.

Signal   End-to-end encrypted private messaging app used on smartphones but also on computers.

Simple Storage Service   Storage service developed by Amazon Web Services.

Single Sign-on   The technology that enables a user to log in to one system and access many others without having to log in to each subsequent system.

Single-tenant   When a customer's use of software-as-a-service is logically or physically separate from other customers.

Slack   Cloud-based chat service.

Smartphone   A device capable of running applications and making phone calls.

Smart TV   Television with Internet capabilities and other computer features.

SMB-grade   Software that is used by small and medium businesses.

SMS-based   Technology that uses SMS.

SOC2   A framework and certification developed by AICPA for cybersecurity.

Social Engineering   The act of tricking a user into an action in order to eventually gain unauthorized access to systems or data.

Software-as-a-service   A type of software product offered in the cloud.

Stakeholders   Individuals who have an interest in the business.

Statement-of-work   A legal document that details specific work, typically not reoccurring, that includes pricing and expected deliverables from said work.

System-on-a-chip   Hardware technology that includes all components of a single computer system in one chip.

Terraform   Software used to create Infrastructure as code.

Texting   The act of sending short messages on smartphones.

Third Party   An organization that is separate from the service provider and customer.

Thunderbird   An email client developed by Mozilla Foundation.

TPRM   Acronym for third-party risk management.

Transport Layer Security A protocol used to encrypt data in transit, typically used in securing web browser traffic.

Trust Criteria The five principals that make up the SOC2 standard.

Twitter Microblogging website.

Ubiquiti Wireless network hardware manufacturer.

UEM Abbreviation of unified endpoint management software.

UK National Cyber Security Centre The organization that governs UK cyber essentials standard.

UL's Cybersecurity Assurance Program Underwriters Laboratory framework for cybersecurity of IoT devices.

Unencrypt Making data readable or useable again through cryptographic functions in conjunction with a secret or key.

Unified Endpoint Management Software to monitor, maintain, and control user devices.

Upsell Selling additional products, services, or solutions to an existing customer.

US-based Location specifics in a contract that dictate where a customer's data will geographically reside.

Username Data that uniquely identifies a user in a system and that is used by that user as part of their credentials to access systems and data.

VC Abbreviation for venture capitalist.

Verizon American telecommunications company providing technology and communications services.

Verizon DBIR An annual report on data breach incidents written by Verizon.

Virtru A cloud-based email encryption software company.

Virtualized A system that is running within another system.

Virtual Local Area Networks Network technology that allows logical separation of devices on the same physical network.

Virtual Private Networks Software capable of encrypting network traffic from point to point.

VMware Large technology company.

VPN Abbreviation of virtual private network.

VSA-Core Cybersecurity and privacy questionnaire developed by VSA.

VSA-Full Cybersecurity and privacy questionnaire developed by VSA.

WannaCry   Ransomware worm that caused billions of dollars in damages in 2017.

Waterfall   A software development methodology.

WeWork   Large co-working space vendor.

Wickr   End-to-end encrypted messaging app designed for enterprise use.

Windows   Operating system developed by Microsoft.

Windows-based   Software designed to run on the Microsoft Windows operating system.

Windows XP   A version of Windows operating system developed by Microsoft.

Word   Word processor software developed by Microsoft.

Xcode   A development environment developed by Apple.

YouTube   Video hosting website.

Yubico   Manufacture of hardware multi-factor authentication devices.

YubiKey   Hardware authentication manufacture.

Index